MENTOR LER

Band 545

Englisch

7./8. Klasse

Keep it up! 1

Ein Übungsprogramm für
Grammatik und Wortschatz 1

Mit ausführlichem Lösungsteil zum Heraustrennen

Mit Lerntipps!

Astrid Stannat
Dieter D'Zenit
Willi Mey †

Mentor Verlag München

In Zusammenarbeit mit Langenscheidt

Über die Autoren:
Astrid Stannat, Studienrätin für Englisch

Dieter D'Zenit, Fachlehrer für Englisch (Hauptschule), Referent in der Lehrerfortbildung

Willi Mey †, Schulamtsdirektor, Referent in der Lehrerfortbildung

Lerntipps:
Astrid Stannat, Studienrätin für Englisch

Redaktion: Eva-Maria Gärtner

Illustrationen: Christiane Hansen, Hamburg,
Susanne Becker, Jutta Bauer, Hamburg

Layout: Barbara Slowik, München

Titelgestaltung: Iris Steiner, München

Umwelthinweis: Gedruckt auf chlorfrei gebleichtem Papier.

Auflage:	6.	5.	4.	3.	Letzte Zahlen
Jahr:	2004	2003	2002	2001	maßgeblich

© 1999 by Mentor Verlag Dr. Ramdohr KG, München

Das Werk und seine Teile sind urheberrechtlich geschützt. Jede Verwertung in anderen als den gesetzlich zugelassenen Fällen bedarf deshalb der vorherigen schriftlichen Einwilligung des Verlages.

Satz/Repro: OK Satz GmbH, Unterschleißheim
Druck: Landesverlag Druckservice, Linz
Printed in Austria · ISBN 3-580-63545-X

Vorwort		5
Benutzerhinweise		6
A	**Die Zeitformen des Verbs**	7
Test		15
Bits & Pieces: Pictures and words		18
B	**Englisch reden? – Kein Problem!**	20
1.	Jemanden kennen lernen	20
2.	Fragen stellen: Welche Fragetypen gibt es?	26
3.	Seine Meinung äußern	32
Test		36
Bits & Pieces: Die Arbeit mit dem Wörterbuch		37
C	**Die Verwendung von *Past Tense* und *Present Perfect***	39
1.	*Simple Past* und *Present Perfect*	40
2.	*Simple Past* und *Past Progressive*	48
3.	Der Gebrauch des *Present Perfect* mit *since* und *for*	50
Test		55
Bits & Pieces: Hören und Sprechen		57
D	**Can, must, may – und ihre Ersatzformen**	59
1.	Das unvollständige Hilfsverb *can*	59
2.	Das unvollständige Hilfsverb *may*	62
3.	Das unvollständige Hilfsverb *must*	64
4.	Die unvollständigen Hilfsverben *can, must, may* und die Zukunft	70
Test		72
Bits & Pieces: Don't be caught speechless		74
E	**Indirekte Rede: Aussagesätze** [+ CHAPTER H.]	76
1.	Die Zeitenfolge in der indirekten Rede	78
2.	Weitere Veränderungen in der indirekten Rede	82
Test		84
Bits & Pieces: How to use the dictionary		86

F   Some – any, much – many: Unbestimmte Pronomen 88
1. *some – any* 88
2. *each – every* 91
3. *much – many – a lot (of)* 92
4. *(a) little – (a) few* 93
Test 94

Bits & Pieces: Reading 96

G   Das Passiv 98
1. Die Zeitformen des Passivs 99
2. Aktiv und Passiv 103
3. Das Passiv in Verbindung mit *can*, *must* und *may* 106
4. Das persönliche Passiv 108
Test 110

Bits & Pieces: Unregelmäßige Verben 112

H   Indirekte Rede: Fragesätze und Befehlssätze 114
1. Fragen in der indirekten Rede 115
2. Befehlssätze in der indirekten Rede 120
Test 125

Bits & Pieces: Rechtschreibung 127

I   Der Genitiv 129
1. Der *s*-Genitiv 129
2. Der *of*-Genitiv 133
3. Der Genitiv ohne nachfolgendes Substantiv 134
4. Der „doppelte" Genitiv 136
Test 138

Lerntipps 140

Quellenverzeichnis 146

Stichwortverzeichnis 147

Lösungsteil 149

Dear friend,

Vielleicht hast du dir – beflügelt von der Arbeit mit den beiden Mentor-Bänden „One, Two, Three … Go!" für die 5. und 6. Jahrgangsstufe – nun auch den vorliegenden Band besorgt. Oder vielleicht bist du eher zufällig in diese Sache hineingeraten! Wie auch immer – wir finden es jedenfalls prima, dass du mit diesem Mentor-Band deine Englischkenntnisse verbessern willst, und uns liegt viel daran, dass du Spaß dabei hast!

Dies ist ein Buch, das gar nicht in der üblichen Weise – nämlich von vorne nach hinten – durchgearbeitet werden will. Du kannst selbst am besten entscheiden, welcher Stoff dir Schwierigkeiten bereitet und daher vorrangig geübt werden sollte. Daneben findest du aber auch genügend Gelegenheit, ganz nach Lust und Laune zu schmökern, auszuprobieren und auf spielerische Weise deine Englischkenntnisse zu erweitern.

Einige Hinweise zum Aufbau des Buches sollen dir helfen, dich zurechtzufinden:

Die Hauptkapitel beschäftigen sich jeweils mit einem bestimmten Aspekt aus den Bereichen Grammatik, Wortschatz und Sprechfertigkeit. Nachdem du dir ein Kapitel herausgesucht hast, solltest du dieses Kapitel auch ganz durcharbeiten. Auf eine kurze Einleitung folgen Regeln, Beispiele, Übersichten und jede Menge *Exercises* und *Games*, die aufeinander aufbauen und daher nicht übersprungen werden sollten.

Das bedeutet aber nicht, dass du das ganze Kapitel an einem Tag durcharbeiten musst! Wenn du das Gefühl hast: „Jetzt geht nichts mehr!", dann mach eine Pause und arbeite später oder am nächsten Tag weiter.

Benutze einen Bleistift, damit du falsche Lösungen leichter korrigieren oder auch die Lösungen wieder ganz ausradieren kannst, um die Übung vielleicht nach einiger Zeit noch einmal zu machen. Schau die Lösungen im Lösungsteil erst nach, <u>nachdem</u> du eine Übung <u>vollständig</u> gemacht hast.

Am Ende jedes Kapitels kannst du anhand eines *Tests* deine Kenntnisse überprüfen. Die Testauswertung findest du gleich im Anschluss. Trage die Anzahl deiner richtigen (und falschen) Lösungen in dein *Personal Scoreboard* ein und lies die entsprechende Bemerkung, die zu deiner Punktzahl passt.

Mit der richtigen Technik lernt es sich bedeutend leichter!

Deshalb findest du auf den *Bits & Pieces*-Seiten, die wir zwischen den Hauptkapiteln eingeschoben haben, viele Anregungen zum Thema Lerntechniken. Lass dich überraschen!

Vorwort

Na, dann kann's jetzt eigentlich losgehen! Auf zwei wichtige Voraussetzungen für gutes Gelingen wollen wir noch hinweisen:

1. der richtige Zeitpunkt: „Bin ich gerade aufnahmefähig und konzentriert?"
2. die richtige Lernumgebung: Richte dir deinen Arbeitsplatz so ein, dass du dich wohl fühlst, aber gleichzeitig konzentriert arbeiten kannst.

Wir hoffen, dass dir die Arbeit mit diesem Mentor-Band Spaß macht und dir Erfolg bringt.

Autoren und Verlag

Übrigens: Das hier ist Fred. Er wird dir in diesem Buch noch oft begegnen. Fred möchte dir beim Englischlernen mit Rat und Tat zur Seite stehen.

Benutzerhinweise

Hier findest du den Hinweis darauf, was du in diesem Kapitel lernen kannst.

Hier findest du eine wichtige Grammatikregel.

Hier erfährst du Wichtiges über Grammatik und Wortschatz.

Exercise: Dies ist entweder eine Aufwärmübung am Anfang eines Kapitels oder eine Übung, in der du das bisher Gelernte anwenden sollst.

Game: Durch Spiele wollen wir dich anregen, frei Englisch zu sprechen.

Test: Hier kannst du überprüfen, ob du alles verstanden hast und auch richtig anwenden kannst.

My personal scoreboard: Hier kannst du dein Testergebnis eintragen.

Der Text dieses Bandes entspricht der neuen Rechtschreibung.

Die Zeitformen des Verbs
The tense forms

A camping holiday

- Have you ever eaten cold spaghetti before?
- I ate my last proper meal four days ago!
- When I get home, I will eat two double cheeseburgers and a large portion of chips!
- At home we often eat ice-cream for dessert.
- After Tim had eaten three apple-pies with ice-cream last week-end, he felt sick.

In diesem Kapitel kannst du die Bildung der verschiedenen Zeiten wiederholen.

Um auszudrücken, dass sich etwas in der Vergangenheit ereignet hat, für die Gegenwart zutrifft oder sich in der Zukunft abspielen wird, hast du die Auswahl unter zahlreichen verschiedenen Verbformen. Aber wer die Wahl hat, hat manchmal auch die Qual! Hier hast du die einmalige Gelegenheit, dir einen Überblick über die am häufigsten verwendeten Zeiten *(Tenses)* zu verschaffen.

Schau dir den folgenden Zeitstrahl an – er soll dir helfen, die verschiedenen Zeiten einzuordnen:

Vergangenheit		Gegenwart		Zukunft
Past Perfect	Simple Past	Present Perfect	Simple Present	Future
Tim had eaten	I ate	I have eaten	we eat	I will eat

Das **Present Perfect** steht zwischen Vergangenheit und Gegenwart, weil es beide Aspekte in sich trägt. – Damit beschäftigen wir uns später noch ausführlicher.

Zunächst wollen wir uns aber genauer ansehen, **wie** die verschiedenen Zeiten **gebildet werden**.

Zu jedem unregelmäßigen Verb findest du im Wörterbuch 3 Formen. Die erste Verbform ist der Infinitiv *(Infinitive)*, die 2. Form ist die Form der Vergangenheit *(Past Tense)* und die 3. Form ist das Partizip *(Past Participle)*. Diese 3. Form brauchst du, um das *Present Perfect* und das *Past Perfect* zu bilden. Bei den regelmäßigen Verben stehen die 2. und die 3. Form nicht dabei, weil sie immer gleich gebildet werden.

! Hier siehst du die regelmäßigen Verbformen. In der 2. und 3. Form wird einfach *-ed* angehängt.

1. Form	2. Form	3. Form
(Infinitive)	*(Past Tense)*	*(Past Participle)*
(to) stay	stayed	stayed
(to) call	called	called
(to) move	moved	moved
(to) clean	cleaned	cleaned

Endet ein Verb im Infinitiv auf **Konsonant + y**, dann wird in der 2. und 3. Form *-ied* aus der Endung:

(to) empty	emptied	emptied

Endet ein Verb auf einem stummen *-e*, dann wird nur noch ein *-d* angehängt:

(to) move	moved	moved

Nach einem kurzen Vokal wird der auslautende Konsonant verdoppelt:

(to) stop	stopped	stopped

! Bei den unregelmäßigen Verben ist es etwas komplizierter – am besten prägst du dir gleich alle drei Formen des jeweiligen Verbs ein; dann hast du bei der Bildung der Zeiten keine Probleme:

(to) eat	ate	eaten
(to) see	saw	seen
(to) go	went	gone
(to) begin	began	begun
(to) throw	threw	thrown

Zeitformen des Verbs

In der folgenden Übung sind die Regeln für die Bildung der verschiedenen Zeiten aufgeführt. Trage die richtige Bezeichnung für die jeweilige Zeit ein:

Exercise A 1

Past Perfect ?? *Present Perfect ??* *Simple Present ??* *Simple Past ??* *Future I ??*

---

regelmäßige Verben: *-ed* an die Grundform unregelmäßige Verben: 2. Form	*will* + Grundform des Verbs im Mündlichen: *'ll* + Grundform
Grundform des Verbs 3. Pers. Singular *(he, she, it)*: *-s* wird angehängt	*had* + 3. Form (*-ed* oder unregelmäßige Form)
I, you, we, they *have* + 3. Form he, she, it *has* + 3. Form	

Zeitformen des Verbs

Exercise A 2 Hier kannst du zeigen, wie fit du im Hinblick auf unregelmäßige Verben bist! Zeichne die fehlenden Luftballonschnüre, so dass jeweils alle drei Formen eines Verbs bei Fred zusammenlaufen.

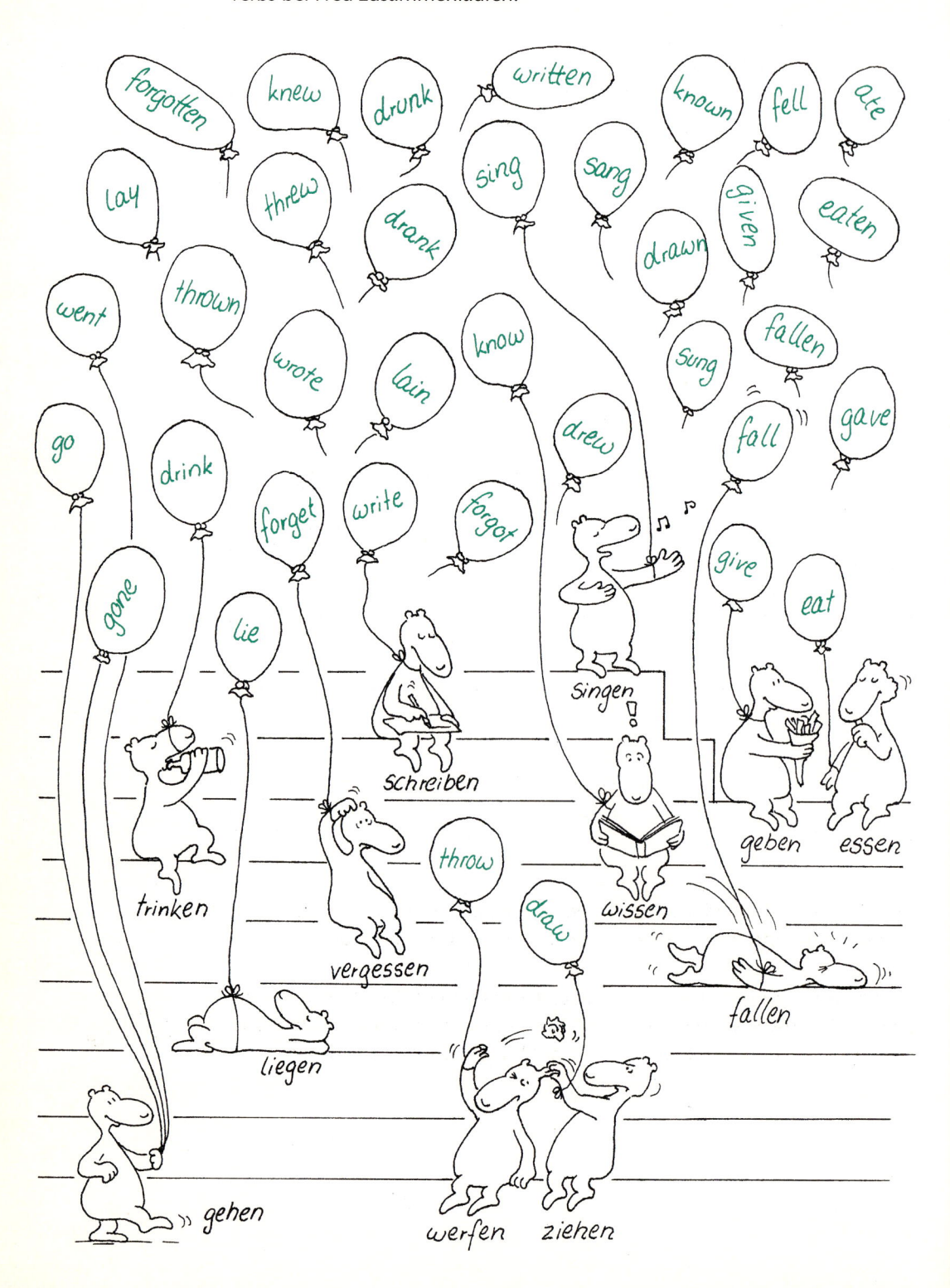

Zeitformen des Verbs

In der folgenden Tabelle kommen sowohl regelmäßige als auch unregelmäßige Verben in verschiedenen Personen vor. Ergänze die fehlenden Formen:

Exercise A 3

Past Perfect	Simple Past	Present Perfect	Simple Present	Future
	he played			
		she has gone		
I had opened				
			we come	
	I tried			
				he will write
she had seen				
			they spend	
	she read			
		it has rained		

Hier noch eine Übung für Schnellsprecher. Damit kannst du die Bildung von *Simple Present* und *Present Perfect* im schnellen Wechsel trainieren.

Für den Anfang ist es vielleicht hilfreich, wenn du die Sätze anhand der gegebenen Stichwörter aufschreibst. Im zweiten Durchgang kannst du versuchen, die Kettensätze mündlich – und möglichst schnell – zu formulieren.

Exercise A 4

Zeitformen des Verbs

> I wake up at six.
>
> When I've woken up, I get up.
>
> When I've got up, I wash.
>
> When I've ..., I ...
>
> When I've ..., I ...

> Hier sind die Stichwörter:
> wake up at six – get up – wash – put on my clothes – go downstairs into the kitchen – have breakfast – go into the garden – play football – read a book – write a letter – buy a pound of apples – feed the horses – draw a picture – sing a song – repair the car – tell a story – watch TV – go to bed

Und nun bilde eine neue Reihe von Kettensätzen:

Tom wakes up at six. When he has woken up, he gets up. When ...

Na, das klappt ja schon ganz prima! Und weil du die Bildung der verschiedenen Zeiten so gut beherrschst, können wir uns jetzt den verneinten Formen und den Fragen zuwenden. Hier ist in bestimmten Zeiten eine Umschreibung mit *do* nötig. In anderen Zeiten brauchst du *do* nicht, weil du die Verbformen mit einem Hilfsverb: *have* oder *will* gebildet hast. Dann kannst du dieses Hilfsverb benutzen, um verneinte Sätze und Fragen zu bilden. Und damit du auch hier einen klaren Kopf behältst, zunächst die Übersicht:

Verneinte Sätze:

Vergangenheit		Gegenwart		Zukunft
Past Perfect	*Simple Past*	*Present Perfect*	*Simple Present*	*Future*
she hadn't eaten	she didn't eat	she hasn't eaten	she doesn't eat	she won't eat
we hadn't eaten	we didn't eat	we haven't eaten	we don't eat	we won't eat

Umschreibung mit **didn't** ↑ ↑ **don't/doesn't**

Die langen Formen lauten:

| we had not eaten | we did not eat | we have not eaten | we do not eat | we will not eat |

Zeitformen des Verbs

Vervollständige nun die folgende Tabelle:

Past Perfect	Simple Past	Present Perfect	Simple Present	Future
			we don't know	
it hadn't helped				
		she hasn't given		
				you won't win
	I didn't move			
he hadn't forgotten				
				they won't buy
		we haven't seen		
	she didn't spend			
			I don't sleep	

Exercise A 5

Ähnlich wie bei den verneinten Sätzen ist auch bei einigen Fragen eine Umschreibung mit *do* erforderlich:

Fragen:

Vergangenheit		Gegenwart		Zukunft
Past Perfect	*Simple Past*	*Present Perfect*	*Simple Present*	*Future*
had you eaten?	did you eat?	have you eaten?	do you eat?	will you eat?
had she eaten?	did she eat?	has she eaten?	does she eat?	will she eat?

↑ Umschreibung ↑
did   *do/does*

Zeitformen des Verbs   **13**

Exercise A 6

Auch Fragen in den verschiedenen Zeiten kannst du wieder mit einer Tabelle üben:

Past Perfect	Simple Past	Present Perfect	Simple Present	Future
			does he like?	
	did you catch?			
had he forgotten?				
				will they go?
		have we hit?		
had they seen?				
				will you tell?
		have I opened?		
			does he take?	
	did she lose?			

Die Verbformen in bejahten und verneinten Sätzen sowie Fragen – wie du sie gerade geübt hast – stellen natürlich nur ein Skelett dar. Jetzt wollen wir versuchen, aus diesen Skeletten richtige Lebewesen entstehen zu lassen, indem wir **ganze Sätze** oder größere Satzzusammenhänge bilden. Dann sehen unsere Verbformen nicht mehr so dürr und klapprig aus!

Zeitformen des Verbs

Du kannst diese Übung schriftlich oder mündlich machen.
Suche dir zehn verschiedene Verbformen aus den drei Tabellen aus und
mache daraus ganze Sätze oder erzähle eine kleine Geschichte!

Exercise A 7

Beispiele:

they spent: Our neighbours spent their holidays in the United States. They sent us a postcard on which you can see the Empire State Building.

we haven't seen: We haven't seen our grandparents for more than a year now. They live in Australia.

does he take? Does your son often take things apart? – Yes, he wants to explore everything. But he's not very keen on putting things together again. That's why we can't use our TV set, the toaster, and the hoover[1] at the moment!

1 Staubsauger

Test

Wie lauten die drei Formen der folgenden unregelmäßigen Verben?
(Je 1 Punkt für jede richtige Form, also max. 3 Punkte pro Verb)

nehmen

verstecken

wissen

lesen

fallen

machen

bauen

erzählen

kaufen

fühlen

Zeitformen des Verbs **15**

Forme die folgenden Sätze um. Behalte aber die jeweilige Zeit bei.
(Je 2 Punkte für jeden richtigen Satz)

Beispiel:

(bejahter Satz)   Michael called me yesterday.
(verneinter Satz)   *Michael didn't call me yesterday.*

(Frage)   Will we arrive at the airport in time?
(bejahter Satz)   ....

(verneinter Satz)   Judy doesn't get up at five o'clock every day.
(bejahter Satz)   ....

(Frage)   Have the Greens sold their car?
(verneinter Satz)   ....

(bejahter Satz)   Brian has pancakes for breakfast every day.
(verneinter Satz)   ....

(verneinter Satz)   They hadn't met before.
(Frage)   ....

(Frage)   Did Janet buy that dress in New York?
(bejahter Satz)   ....

Zeitformen des Verbs

Testauswertung

My personal scoreboard:

42–34 "right" scores:
With your excellent result you've won the gold medal!

33–22 "right" scores:
That's a pretty good result! You'll get the silver medal for it! If you want to go for gold, revise the irregular verb forms and/or the tenses you have difficulties with!

21–0 "right" scores:
Maybe you haven't done enough warming-up exercises!
Do all the exercises in this chapter and don't forget to revise the irregular verb forms!

Pictures and words

It is much easier to learn words in combination with a picture. Here is an example:

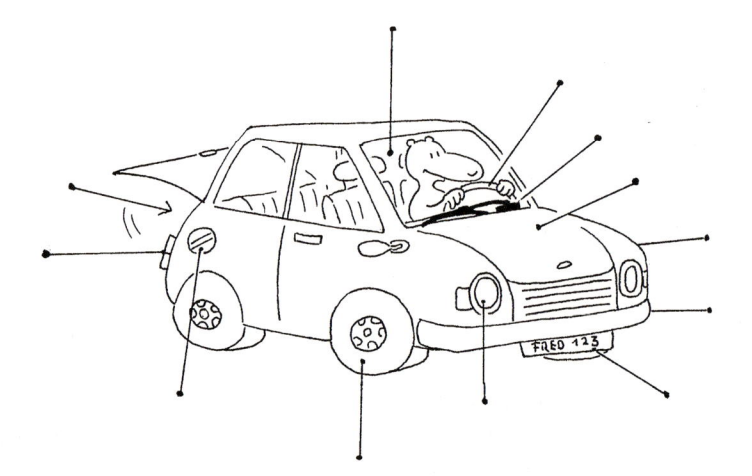

If you make a photocopy of this page, you can put the picture and the words into an envelope and use them more than once.

Cut out the words and put them in the right place:

windscreen	bumper	front lights	bonnet
mudguard	boot	petrol tank	tyre
steering wheel	rear lights	number plate	windscreen wipers

Whenever you put a word next to the picture of the car, say what this part of the car is used for.

Example:

You/I/We can put our luggage or shopping bags into the **boot**.

Further activities: You can try the same with other pictures.

Here are some suggestions – add more words, make a photocopy and cut the words out. Then stick them onto the pictures.

deck-chair	clouds
bathing shorts	sunshade
sunglasses	umbrella
puddle	

You could try to make up little stories. Start like this:

1. A few weeks ago something funny happened. Fred was lying in a deck-chair …
2. Last weekend Fred and some friends of his wanted to go to the cinema. They had just set off when it started to rain …

Pictures and words   19

B   Englisch reden? – Kein Problem!
Talking in English? – No problem!

1. Jemanden kennen lernen
Getting to know somebody

In diesem Kapitel übst du, wie man sich auf Englisch unterhält, Fragen stellt, telefoniert und diskutiert.

Fred hat im Urlaub auf dem Campingplatz ein nettes Mädchen kennen gelernt. Sie heißt Julie und ist Australierin. Die beiden stellen sich gegenseitig viele Fragen.

Match the questions and the answers.
Male die Sprechblasen in verschiedenen Farben an und verwende jeweils die gleiche Farbe für eine Frage und die dazugehörige Antwort.

Exercise B 1

- What's your name?
- Can you play the didgeridoo?[1]
- I'm from Adelaide. That's in the south of Australia.
- Well, I'm quite good at languages, but maths isn't my cup of tea!
- What are your hobbies?
- The "Spice Girls" are my favourite group but I also like Australian bands like "Men at Work".
- What kind of music do you like?
- I'm fourteen.
- I like reading, swimming and waterskiing.
- Are you good at school?
- You mean that traditional Aborigine instrument? No, I'm afraid I can't.
- How old are you?
- My name is Fred.
- Where are you from?

What would you answer if somebody asked you all those questions?

Englisch reden

Stell dir vor, du lernst im Urlaub ein Mädchen oder einen Jungen kennen, das/der nicht Deutsch spricht. Überlege dir fünf Fragen, die du ihm stellen würdest.
Lies erst weiter, wenn du diese fünf Fragen formuliert hast!

Vielleicht findest du die eine oder andere deiner Fragen in der folgenden Übung wieder. Ordne die deutschen Formulierungen den englischen Fragen zu:

Exercise B 2

Wenn du wissen möchtest, ob das Mädchen oder der Junge ...	**Wie müsstest du dann fragen?**
1. eine(n) Brieffreund(in) hat,	Have you got a pet?
2. gerne Reisen unternimmt,	Would you like to go to the beach?
3. schon mal in Deutschland war,	Have you got school in the afternoon?
4. eine gute Sportlerin/ein guter Sportler ist,	Would you like to keep in touch with me?
5. ein Haustier hat,	Have you ever been to Germany?
6. in einer großen Stadt wohnt,	Are you good at sports?
7. gerne Techno-Musik hört,	Do you like travelling?
8. Geschwister hat,	Have you ever played truant?
9. am Nachmittag Schule hat,	Do you live in a big city?
10. schon mal die Schule geschwänzt hat[1],	Have you got a pen-friend?
11. mit dir zum Strand gehen will,	Do you like listening to Techno music?
12. mit dir in Verbindung bleiben möchte.	Have you got any brothers or sisters?

1 (to) play truant

Lies die englischen Fragen einige Male laut vor dich hin.
Decke nun die rechte Seite zu und formuliere die entsprechenden Fragen von 1 bis 12.

Englisch reden

Da du dich mit deiner neuen Freundin bzw. deinem neuen Freund prima verstehst, möchtest du sie/ihn auch mal einladen, mit dir etwas zu unternehmen oder sie/ihn um einen Gefallen bitten. Fred zeigt dir, was man in solchen Situationen sagen kann:

Vorschlag

Du willst deiner Freundin/deinem Freund vorschlagen mit dir Minigolf zu spielen.

- Would you like to play minigolf with me in the afternoon?
- How about playing minigolf after lunch?
- Let's play minigolf in the afternoon!

Würdest du gerne …?

Wie wär's mit …/ wenn wir …?

Lass uns …!
Spielen wir doch …!

Bitte

Du bittest sie/ihn, dir etwas zu schicken.

- Could you please send me an Australian youth magazine?
- It would be really nice if you could send me an Australian youth magazine!
- Do you think you could send me an Australian youth magazine?

Könnest du bitte …?

Es wäre sehr nett, wenn du …!

Könntest du vielleicht …?

Einladung

Du möchtest deine Freundin/deinen Freund einladen, dich in den nächsten Ferien zu besuchen.

- Why don't you come and visit me in the next holidays?
- Would you like to visit me in the next holidays?
- I'd be very pleased if you visited me in the next holidays!

Warum besuchst du mich nicht …?

Würdest du gerne …?

Ich würde mich sehr freuen, wenn …!

Englisch reden

Tipp

Für deutsche Muttersprachler wirken derartige Äußerungen im Englischen manchmal übertrieben höflich. Umgekehrt empfinden englische *native speakers* deutsche Sprecher gelegentlich als sehr direkt, barsch oder sogar unhöflich. Sprachliche Umgangsformen sind einfach von Land zu Land verschieden. Deshalb unser Tipp: Drücke dich im Englischen lieber etwas höflicher aus – das verringert die Zahl der Fettnäpfchen, in die man treten kann, ganz beträchtlich!

Beispiel:

Give me the butter!	Ziemlich unhöflich.
Can I have the butter?!	Nicht sehr höflich.
Can I have the butter, please?	Schon besser! Bei Freunden und Familienmitgliedern akzeptabel.
Could / May *I have the butter, please?*	Höflich.
Could / Would *you please pass me the butter?!*	Noch höflicher.

Englisch reden

Exercise B 3

Now it's your turn:
What would you say in the following situations?

1. Du möchtest Freunde zu deiner Geburtstagsfeier einladen.

   ....

   ....

1 etw. ausleihen – **to borrow**
jemanden etw. leihen – **to lend**

2. Du bittest einen Jungen, dir seine Luftmatratze zu leihen[1].

   ....

   ....

3. Du schlägst deinen Eltern vor, nächstes Jahr in Irland Urlaub zu machen.

   ....

   ....

4. Du bittest deinen Tischnachbarn, dir das Salz herüberzureichen.

   ....

   ....

5. Du schlägst deiner Freundin/deinem Freund vor, abends in die Hotelsdisko zu gehen.

   ....

   ....

6. Deine Eltern möchten deine Freundin/deinen Freund und ihre/seine Eltern zum Abendessen einladen.

   ....

   ....

Wenn man jemandem direkt gegenübersteht, ist die Verständigung immer noch leichter als am Telefon. Telefonieren in der Fremdsprache ist für viele eine Herausforderung, auf die sie gerne verzichten! Dabei ist es gar nicht so schwer, wenn man einige typische Ausdrücke beherrscht!

Englisch reden

Fred möchte seinen deutschen Freund Jörg zum Grillen einladen. Die einzelnen Teile des Telefongesprächs sind etwas durcheinander geraten. Kannst du sie in die richtige Reihenfolge (1–12) bringen?

Exercise B 4

- (1) Hello, Mrs Winkler! This is Fred speaking. Can I talk to Jörg?
- ( ) Thank you.
- ( ) Hello, Jörg. How are you?
- ( ) Oh, what a pity! At what time is the match?
- ( ) You could come after the match, couldn't you?
- ( ) That's great! I hope your team will win. I'll keep my fingers crossed for you![1]
- ( ) I'm alright. Listen, Jörg. We are planning to have a barbecue next Saturday. I'd like you to come, too. Are you free on Saturday evening?
- ( ) See you on Saturday. Bye!

1 Ich drücke dir die Daumen!

- ( ) Hello, Fred. I'll go and get him. Hold on!

- ( ) At five o'clock.
- ( ) I'm fine, thanks. And you?
- ( ) Yes, if that's o. k. with you.
- ( ) Hello, Fred. It's Jörg here.
- ( ) Oh, Fred, could you speak a little more slowly, please? Well, I have a football match on Saturday.
- ( ) Thank you, Fred! I'm sure that'll help! Thanks for ringing and see you on Saturday then!

Englisch reden 25

In dem Gespräch kommen einige typische Ausdrücke vor, die man häufig am Telefon verwendet. Schreibe sie neben die jeweiligen deutschen Übersetzungen:

Hier ist …/Hier spricht …   a) ....
   b) ....

Kann ich … sprechen?   ....

Bleib dran!   ....

Könntest du bitte etwas langsamer sprechen?   ....
   ....

Wie geht's dir?   ....

Mir geht's gut.   a) ....
   b) ....

Hast du am Samstag Zeit?   ....

Danke, dass du angerufen hast.   ....

Bis Samstag!   ....

Auch hier ist wichtig: Lies die Ausdrücke mehrmals laut! Später kannst du als Wiederholung die englischen Ausdrücke zudecken und überprüfen, ob du sie noch alle weißt.

B 2. Fragen stellen: Welche Fragetypen gibt es?
Asking questions: Types of questions

Im ersten Abschnitt dieses Kapitels hast du geübt, in verschiedenen Gesprächssituationen zurechtzukommen. Es kamen eine ganze Reihe von Fragen vor, die wir jetzt noch einmal genauer unter die Lupe nehmen wollen. Welche Arten von Fragen werden häufig verwendet? Wie werden sie gebildet?

Stell dir vor, es ist Abend. Du bist gerade auf dem Heimweg und triffst unterwegs im Park einen Außerirdischen. Würdest du ihm nicht gerne ein paar Fragen stellen? Fred ist das wirklich passiert – und er war geistesgegenwärtig genug, das seltsame Wesen gleich anzusprechen.

Vervollständige die folgenden Fragen und Kurzantworten.
Diese Hilfsverben stehen dabei zur Auswahl:

~~do~~ – will – may – are – would – can – did – could – have – do

Exercise B 5

_Do_	you understand me?	Yes, I	_do_ .
....	I ask you some questions?	Yes, you	....
....	you from Mars?	No, I	....
....	you come by spacecraft?	No, I	....
....	your parents know where you are?	Yes, they	....
....	you got any friends here?	Yes, I	....
....	you like something to eat?	No, thank you.	
....	you please tell me something about your planet?	Yes, of course.	
....	you go back to your planet soon?	No, I	....

In fact, I'm going to a fancy-dress ball at my friend's house!

Na, man kann sich ja mal irren!

Englisch reden

Freds Fragen fangen zwar alle unterschiedlich an, aber es handelt sich doch immer um den gleichen Fragetyp. Fred hat ausschließlich **Entscheidungsfragen** *(yes/no questions)* gestellt; die Antworten lauten immer „Ja" oder „Nein". Im Englischen steht *Yes* oder *No* fast nie allein, sondern meist als Teil einer so genannten „Kurzantwort": Das Hilfsverb aus der Frage wird hier wieder aufgegriffen und bejaht oder verneint. Manchmal stehen auch andere Formulierungen wie *Yes, of course* oder *No, thank you*.

Sehen wir uns nun etwas genauer an, wie Entscheidungsfragen gebildet werden.

Can   I   ask you some questions?
Did   you   come by spacecraft?
Have   you   got any friends here?

Wenn nicht schon ein Hilfsverb im Satz vorhanden ist, muss mit *do/does* in der Gegenwart bzw. *did* in der Vergangenheit umschrieben werden.

Zur Erinnerung:

Aussagesatz: **Frage:**

I like pizza.   *Do you like pizza?*
Peter likes pancakes.   *Does Peter like pancakes?*

In der **3. Person Singular** steht **in der Gegenwart** ein *-s*!

They came by train.   *Did they come by train?*
Bob came by train.   *Did Bob come by train?*

Das Verb steht bei Fragen mit *do/does/did* **immer in der Grundform**.

Exercise B 6

Formuliere Entscheidungsfragen mit *Do…?/Does…?* oder *Did…?*

1. Jack/live/in London — *Does Jack live in London?*

2. I/lock/the door/last night

3. your brother/speak/Italian

4. you/go out/last Saturday

5. the Millers/spend their holidays/ in Florida/last year

6. you/always/get up/so early

7. your parents/like/dogs

8. Jenny/do well/in her last English test

Englisch reden

Game

Für das folgende Ratespiel benötigst du eine(n) oder mehrere Mitspieler(innen).

One of the players chooses

a person,　　　**an animal,**　　　**a thing,**　　　**or a place.**

The other player(s) have to ask questions in order to find out what it is.

Here is an example:

Mike starts: O. K., I've got it – it's a thing.

Judy: Have you got it in your house?	Yes, we have.
Fred: Is it bigger than a football?	No, it isn't.
Judy: Do you need it for school?	No, I don't.
Fred: Is it a toy?	No, it isn't.
Judy: Is it part of the furniture?	No, it isn't.
Fred: Can you eat it?	No, you can't!
Judy: Has everybody got such a thing in the house?	Yes, almost everybody.
Fred: Do you need it for cooking or eating?	No, you don't.
Judy: Do you have it in the bathroom?	Yes, I do.
Is it a toothbrush?	Bingo! Yes, it is.
	Now it's your turn!

Englisch reden

Bisher hatten wir es immer mit Entscheidungsfragen zu tun. Es gibt aber noch eine weitere wichtige Gruppe von Fragen, die darauf abzielen, dass der Fragende bestimmte Informationen erhält – **Fragesätze mit Fragepronomen**, zum Beispiel:

how long – how many – who (wer) – who (wen) – what – when – where – what colour – what kind of – why – how often – how much

Fill in the right pronoun:
Der berühmte Detektiv Frederic Watson führt gerade wichtige Ermittlungen durch.

Exercise B 7

_____ is that man? – Charles Breakneck!

_____ did you last see him? – Last Friday.

_____ was that? – In the Penguin Bar.

_____ was he wearing? – A coat, I think.

_____ coat? – A leather coat.

_____ ? – Black.

_____ did he stay there? – The whole evening, until one o'clock, I think.

_____ money did he spend there? – I don't know, but I'm sure it was more than £ 100.

_____ people were there that night? – Oh, it was quite crowded, more than 50, I think.

_____ do you normally go there? – Twice a week.

_____ do you go there? – I like the atmosphere. And I like to meet people.

_____ do you meet there? – Friends.

Auch für **Fragesätze mit Fragepronomen** gilt:

Sätze, in denen kein Hilfsverb vorkommt, werden in der Regel mit *do/does/did* umschrieben.

Achtung bei *Who/What...?*

Who knows that man?
(Wer kennt...?)
What stands in the middle of...?
(Was steht...?)

Fragt man mit *Who...?* oder *What...?* nach dem **Subjekt**, wird **nicht** mit *do/does/did* umschrieben.

Who did you meet last Friday?
(Wen hast du ... getroffen?)
What did you see?
(Was hast du gesehen?)

Fragt man mit *Who...?* oder *What...?* nach dem **Objekt**, wird wie gewohnt mit *do/does/did* umschrieben.

Frage nach den unterstrichenen Satzteilen.
Beispiel: Ann met Richard at a party. a) Who met Richard at a party?
                                       b) Who did Anne meet at a party?

1. A fifteen-year-old boy saw the two robbers at Victoria Station.

    a) ....

    b) ....

2. The apple hit my teacher on the head.

    a) ....

    b) ....

3. All the pupils like Mrs Brown.

    a) ....

    b) ....

4. Helen often sees flying saucers in her garden.

    a) ....

    b) ....

5. Judith loves Matthew.

    a) ....

    b) ....

6. The detective followed the black limousine.

    a) ....

    b) ....

Exercise B 8

Exercise B 9

In den folgenden Übungen sind alle Fragetypen vertreten, die du bisher geübt hast.

Hast du Lust, dich mal als Krimiautor zu versuchen? Frederic Holmes arbeitet an einem neuen Fall. Formuliere seine Fragen und erfinde Antworten dazu. Schreibe den Dialog auf ein gesondertes Blatt.

Holmes will von einem wichtigen Zeugen wissen

wo er wohnt,
wo er gestern Abend war,
wer ihn dort gesehen hat,
wie lange er dort geblieben ist,
wo sein Autoschlüssel ist,
ob er die Frau auf dem Foto kennt,
wo sie wohnt,
wann er sie zum letzten Mal gesehen hat.

B 3. Seine Meinung äußern
Expressing one's opinion

In einer „normalen" Unterhaltung stellt man nicht nur Fragen bzw. gibt Antworten; man tauscht auch Erfahrungen und Gedanken aus. So wie die beiden Teenager, die sich gerade über das Fernsehen unterhalten:

Exercise B 10

Es gehören je eine Äußerung und eine Erwiderung zusammen. Verbinde sie mit einer Linie oder male die zusammengehörenden Sprechblasen mit der gleichen Farbe aus.

If you ask me – people watch too much television!

Oh no, that's not true! I really enjoy watching "Roseanne".

Well, of course, but on the other hand, you wouldn't want to have pay TV only, or would you?

I agree with you.

Neither do I!

When the weather is nice, I don't like sitting in front of the goggle-box[2].

In my opinion all those sitcoms[1] on TV are complete rubbish!

I think there shouldn't be any commercials on TV.

1 sitcom: situation comedy – *lustige Familienserie*
2 ugs. *Glotze*

Hier findest du einige Ausdrücke, mit deren Hilfe du deine Meinung bzw. Zustimmung oder Widerspruch äußern kannst:

Wortliste

So äußerst du deine Meinung:

If you ask me …	Wenn du mich fragst …
I think …	Ich denke/meine …
What I think is that …	Ich meine, dass …
In my opinion …	Meiner Meinung nach …
I'm sure (that) …	Ich bin mir sicher, (dass) …
As far as I know …	Soviel ich weiß …
I'm (absolutely) convinced that …	Ich bin (absolut) überzeugt, dass …

So stimmst du deinem Gesprächspartner zu:

That's right/true.	Das stimmt. Das ist richtig/wahr.
I think so, too.	Das denke ich auch.
That's just what I think.	Genau das denke ich auch.
Yes, of course.	Ja, natürlich.
So do I.	Ich auch.
Neither do I.	Ich auch nicht.
Exactly.	Stimmt genau.
I agree with you.	Ich bin deiner Meinung.
That's a good point/idea.	Das ist ein gutes Argument/ein guter Gedanke.

So widersprichst du deinem Gesprächspartner:

O. K., but don't you think …?	Gut, aber meinst du nicht …?
Yes, but on the other hand …	Ja, aber andererseits …
I'm sorry but I don't agree.	Es tut mir Leid, aber ich bin nicht deiner Meinung.
I don't think so.	Ich sehe das anders.
That's not true.	Das stimmt nicht.
I just can't agree with you.	Da kann ich dir einfach nicht zustimmen!
On the contrary …	Im Gegenteil …
Come on!	Ach geh!
Rubbish!	Quatsch! Blödsinn!

Englisch reden

Exercise B 11

Jetzt ist deine Meinung gefragt.
Nimm zu den folgenden Aussagen (mündlich) Stellung:

It's good to learn a foreign language.	No family should have more than one car.	Fast food is unhealthy.
German television is excellent.	Homework is necessary.	Riding a motorbike is dangerous.
Girls shouldn't play football.	German pupils should wear school uniforms.	Women should get equal pay for equal work.

Aus dieser Übung wird ein spannendes Lernspiel, wenn du einen Mitspieler/eine Mitspielerin findest.
Kennst du *Tic-Tac-Toe*? Das ist ein Spiel und geht so:

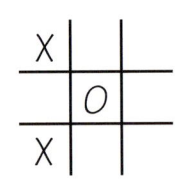

```
X |   |  
--+---+--
  | O |  
--+---+--
X |   |  
```

Ein Mitspieler/eine Mitspielerin malt Kreuze, der/die andere malt Kreise. Es wird ausgelost, wer anfangen darf. Das Gitter ist zunächst leer. Der erste Spieler setzt sein Zeichen in eines der neun Felder; dann ist der andere Spieler dran. Ziel ist es, eine Dreierreihe (senkrecht, waagerecht oder diagonal) voll zu bekommen.
Die Spieler dürfen ihr Symbol erst setzen, wenn sie etwas zu der Äußerung gesagt haben, die in dem betreffenden Feld steht!

Beim nächsten Durchgang fängt der andere Mitspieler an. Ihr könnt euch natürlich andere Äußerungen/Behauptungen überlegen – dann lässt sich das Spiel beliebig oft wiederholen. Und nicht vergessen: Erst nach einer vollständigen, richtigen Äußerung darf ein Kreuz bzw. Kreis gesetzt werden!

Zum Abschluss ein kleines Streitgespräch. Übersetze, was sich die beiden Kontrahenten zu sagen haben:

Exercise B 12

School holidays are too long!

1. Meiner Meinung nach sind drei Monate Schulferien zu lang!

2. Da bin ich anderer Ansicht! Kinder und Jugendliche brauchen diese Zeit, um sich zu erholen.

3. Soviel ich weiß, schlafen (doch) die meisten Schüler im Unterricht. Ich finde, das reicht!

4. Das finde ich aber nicht! Ein Schultag ist wirklich anstrengend, und danach müssen die Schüler (noch) ihre Hausaufgaben machen.

5. Ach was! Es ist keine Schule am Wochenende, und alle paar Wochen sind Ferien. Die Kids wissen doch gar nicht, was sie mit ihrer Freizeit anfangen sollen.

6. Das stimmt nicht. Wir brauchen einfach Zeit für unsere Familie, Freunde und Hobbys. Ich bin mir sicher, dass Sie auch nicht jeden Tag arbeiten wollen!

Bestimmt bist du jetzt mit uns der Meinung: Englisch reden – kein Problem! Den abschließenden Test schaffst du sicher mühelos!

Englisch reden 35

Test

1. Frage Pete,
(Je 2 Punkte für jede richtige Frage)

1. ob er Amerikaner ist.
2. wann er morgens aufsteht.
3. wo er wohnt.
4. ob er dir sein Fahrrad leihen könnte.
5. was er letzten Samstag getan hat.
6. wer „Frankenstein" geschrieben hat.
7. ob er schon mal auf Malta war.
8. wo sein Bruder arbeitet.

2. Übersetze die folgenden Äußerungen zum Thema: School uniforms
(Je 2 Punkte für jede richtige Äußerung)

1. Soviel ich weiß, sind die meisten Schuluniformen dunkelblau, grau oder dunkelgrün.
2. Meiner Meinung nach sollte jeder selbst entscheiden können, was er/sie anziehen will.
3. Genau das denke ich auch. Wenn du mich fragst: Schuluniformen sehen langweilig aus.
4. Ja, aber andererseits ist die Schule keine Disko! Viele Mädchen und Jungs verbringen Stunden vor dem Kleiderschrank!
5. Da stimme ich dir voll zu! Für viele Kids sind Klamotten extrem wichtig – zu wichtig!

Testauswertung

My personal scoreboard:

26–20 "right" scores:
Congratulations! Talking in English is no problem at all for you.

19–13 "right" scores:
Well done! You just need a little more practice. Revise the aspects of conversation you still find difficult.

12–0 "right" scores:
Are you being serious? Have you done **all** the exercises in this chapter? Well, then – off you go! You will see: practice makes perfect!

Die Arbeit mit dem Wörterbuch

I got a new bike for my birthday. It has got 14 ? Gänge?

Bestimmt hast du diese Erfahrung auch schon gemacht: Du willst etwas auf Englisch sagen oder schreiben, aber du weißt ein bestimmtes Wort nicht.

Auch wenn du kein Wörterbuch zur Hand hast, solltest du nicht verzweifeln. Du kannst versuchen, das Wort zu umschreiben, das dir fehlt. Mehr dazu auf den *Bits & Pieces*-Seiten *Don't be caught speechless*.

Manchmal hast du aber mehr Zeit, z. B. wenn du deine Hausaufgaben machst oder einen Brief schreibst, und kannst im Wörterbuch nachschlagen. Oder du willst einfach wissen, wie das Wort nun eigentlich auf Englisch heißt, das du in der Unterhaltung so dringend gebraucht hättest.

Jetzt wollen wir Antje, die das Wort für Gänge beim Fahrrad sucht, tatkräftig unterstützen. In einem Wörterbuch kommen immer wieder bestimmte Abkürzungen, Symbole und Zeichen vor, und es ist sehr wichtig, ihre Bedeutung zu kennen. Hier der Wörterbucheintrag zu Gang:

Stichwort — **Gang** 1. (≈ *Gangart*) walk; **seine Gangart** the way he walks 2. (≈ *Weg*) way 3. (≈ *Flur*) corridor 4. *im Flugzeug usw.*: aisle [⚠ aıl] 5. (≈ *Bogengang*) arcade [ɑːˈkeɪd] 6. *beim Essen*: course [kɔːs]; **Essen mit drei Gängen** three-course meal 7. *beim Auto*: gear [gɪə]; **zweiter** *usw.* **Gang** second *usw.* gear; **in den zweiten Gang schalten** change (*bes. AE* shift) into second (gear) 8. *anatomisch*: duct, canal [kəˈnæl] 9. (≈ *Verlauf*) course; **der Gang der Dinge** the course of events 10. **etwas in Gang setzen** (*oder* bringen) *wörtlich und übertragen* get* something going, start something 11. **in Gang kommen** get* going, get* started 12. **es ist etwas im Gange** *übertragen* there's something going on 13. **die Feier war in vollem Gange, als ...** the party was in full swing when ...

Warndreieck, z. B. bei komplizierter Aussprache

verschiedene Bedeutungen

Sternchen beim unregelmäßigen Verb

kursiv: Verständnishilfen

entspricht

Amerikanisches Englisch (BE = Britisches Englisch)

Aussprache

halbfett kursiv: Wendungen

Das Wort Gang hat viele verschiedene Bedeutungen, aus denen wir einige wichtige herausgreifen wollen. Trage die passende englische Übersetzung ein:

1. Gangart ....
2. Weg ....
3. Flur ....
4. im Flugzeug ....
5. beim Essen ....
6. beim Auto und Fahrrad ....
7. Verlauf ....

Wörtersucharbeit 37

Bits & Pieces

Schlage die folgenden Wörter nach und schreibe die englischen Übersetzungen auf:

Bitte gib mir die Karte.
Please, give me the ...

Postkarte	....
Landkarte	....
Fahrkarte	....
Speisekarte	....

Das ist der letzte Zug.
This is the last ...

Eisenbahn	....
Schachzug	....

Ich kann das Rezept nicht finden.
I can't find the ...

Kochrezept	....
Rezept vom Arzt	....

Er sitzt schon seit Stunden auf dieser Bank.
He has been sitting on this ... for hours.

Geldinstitut	....
Sitzbank	....

Ist dieses Bild von Picasso?
Is that a ... by Picasso?

allgemein	....
Gemälde	....
Foto	....
Zeichnung	....

Wörtersucharbeit

Die Verwendung von *Past Tense* und *Present Perfect*

The use of the past tense and the present perfect

Was du schon immer über Past Tense *und* Present Perfect *wissen wolltest. – In diesem Kapitel lernst du, diese beiden Zeiten richtig zu verwenden.*

Angler catches whale

Mr J. Gallagher, a 43-year-old taxi driver from Stonehaven, was fishing off the pier last Saturday. When he wanted to reel in[1] a fish, he got the shock of his life: he had caught a dead whale which had been drifting[2] in the sea!
"It took me about 45 minutes to pull the whale ashore[3]", Mr Gallagher told our reporter. "I got help from some passers-by[4]. You know, I've been going fishing for more than fifteen years now, but this is the biggest 'fish' I've ever caught!"
As we were told by a marine expert, the whale is 20 feet[5] long. So far nobody knows what caused the death of the whale.

1 (die Angelschnur) einholen
2 treiben
3 an Land
4 Passanten, Vorübergehende
5 ca. 6,10 Meter

Auch in diesem Kapitel stehen verschiedene Zeiten – nämlich das *Past Tense* und *Present Perfect* – im Mittelpunkt. Falls du dir nicht mehr ganz sicher bist, wie diese Zeiten gebildet werden, empfehlen wir dir, zunächst Kapitel A dieses Buches durchzuarbeiten.
Solltest du das bereits getan haben, kannst du gleich mit der ersten Übung loslegen:

Exercise C 1

In dem Zeitungsbericht über den kuriosen Walfang kommen die folgenden Zeiten mindestens einmal vor. Trage in jede Spalte ein Beispiel aus dem Text ein:

Past Perfect (Simple): ....

Past Perfect (Progressive): ....

Past (Simple): ....

Past (Progressive): ....

Present Perfect (Simple): ....

Present Perfect (Progressive): ....

C 1. Simple Past und Present Perfect
Simple past and present perfect

Nehmen wir noch einmal unseren Zeitstrahl zu Hilfe, um das *Simple Past* und das *Present Perfect* voneinander abzugrenzen:

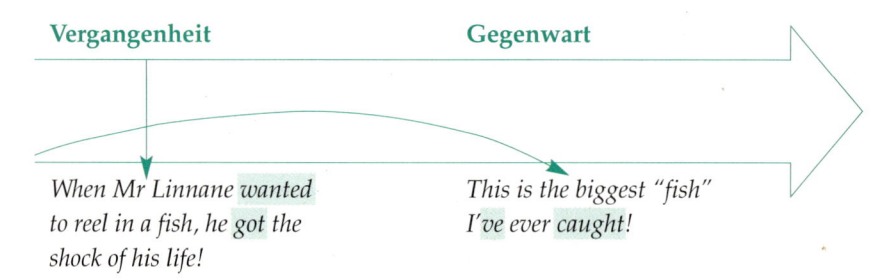

Vergangenheit → **Gegenwart**

When Mr Linnane wanted to reel in a fish, he got the shock of his life!

This is the biggest "fish" I've ever caught!

Regel

Wenn ein Vorgang oder eine Handlung eindeutig in der Vergangenheit passierte, steht das *Past Tense*.

Das *Present Perfect* bildet eine Brücke zwischen Vergangenheit und Gegenwart.

Diese Regeln gelten auch für die jeweilige *Progressive Form*:

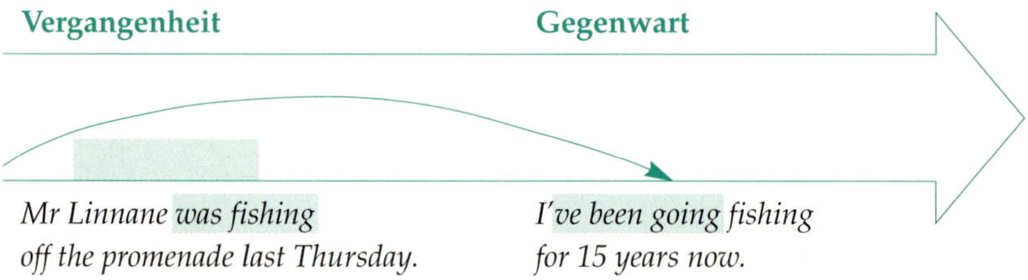

Vergangenheit → **Gegenwart**

Mr Linnane was fishing off the promenade last Thursday.

I've been going fishing for 15 years now.

40 Past Tense und Present Perfect

Es gibt einige **Signalwörter**, die es dir noch leichter machen, dich für die richtige Zeitform zu entscheiden:

Wortliste

Simple Past		*Present Perfect*	
last week	letzte Woche	up to now	bisher,
yesterday	gestern	until now	bis jetzt
two years ago	vor zwei Jahren	till now	
when I was …	als ich … war	yet (in ver-	
when (in Fragen)	wann	neinten Sätzen)	noch nicht
in 1996	(im Jahr) 1996	yet (in Fragen)	schon
		for	seit
		since	seit

Aufgepasst!
Im Deutschen steht in der Umgangssprache bei Erzählungen oft das Perfekt:

Gestern habe ich mit meinem Freund Pete Tennis gespielt.

Die Handlung – das Tennismatch – gehört eindeutig der **Vergangenheit** an, deshalb muss im Englischen *Simple Past* stehen:

Yesterday I played tennis with my friend Pete.

Past Tense und Present Perfect

Zwei Mädchen unterhalten sich über die Ferien, die eine von den beiden in Spanien verbracht hat.

Ergänze die englischen Verbformen und vergiss dabei nicht, dass du bei Berichten über Vergangenes immer das *Past Tense* verwenden musst:

Exercise C 2

Wo seid ihr denn in den Ferien gewesen?

Wir waren in Spanien.

War's schön?

Ja. Wir hatten ein schönes Ferienhaus in der Nähe des Strandes. Vormittags haben wir oft etwas besichtigt und nachmittags sind wir dann an den Strand gegangen und haben Volleyball gespielt oder im Meer gebadet.

Hast du auch nette Leute getroffen?

Ja, da war eine Familie aus Hamburg mit zwei Mädchen. Die eine war 14, die andere 12. Wir haben viel zusammen gemacht.

Wie war das Essen?

Wir haben meistens selbst gekocht. Alle paar Tage sind wir in ein Restaurant gegangen und haben etwas typisch Spanisches gegessen. Nur einmal hatte ich etwas, das mir nicht geschmeckt hat. Sonst war es immer sehr lecker.

Ach, übrigens – vielen Dank für deine Karte! Ich hab sie gestern bekommen.

Erst gestern? Ich hab sie vor mehr als zwei Wochen geschrieben!

– Where (spend) _____ your holidays?

– We (be) _____ in Spain.

– (be) _____ it nice?

– Yes, it was./We (have) _____ a nice holiday home near the beach. In the morning we often (visit) _____ some sights and in the afternoon we (go) _____ to the beach and (play) _____ volleyball or (swim) _____ in the sea.

– (meet) _____ any nice people?

– Yes, there (be) _____ a family from Hamburg with two girls. One (be) _____ 14, the other one (be) _____ 12. We (do) _____ a lot of things together.

– What (be) _____ the food like?

– Most of the time we (cook) _____ our own meals. Every few days we (go) _____ to a restaurant and (eat) _____ some typical Spanish food. Only once I (have) _____ something I (not like) _____. Apart from that it (be) _____ always very tasty.

– By the way – many thanks for your postcard! I (get) _____ it yesterday.

– Only yesterday? I (write) _____ it more than two weeks ago!

Past Tense und Present Perfect

Nachdem du den Lückentext ausgefüllt hast, lies nun den ganzen (englischen) Text noch einmal durch, decke ihn dann ab und versuche den gesamten Dialog ins Englische zu übersetzen. Und nicht vergessen: immer *Past Tense*!

Jetzt wollen wir noch einen Blick auf die Verwendung des *Present Perfect* werfen:

> Bist du schon mal in Spanien gewesen?
>
> Ja, wir waren schon mehrere Male auf Mallorca.
>
> Have you ever been to Spain?
>
> Yes, we've been to Mallorca several times.

Regel

In diesem Beispiel wird eine **allgemeine Frage** gestellt bzw. eine **allgemeine Aussage** gemacht – und zwar **ohne genaue Zeitangabe**. Wenn das **Ergebnis** im Vordergrund steht, verwendest du das *Present Perfect*.

Past Tense und Present Perfect 43

Dazu gleich eine Übung:

At a travel agency

Exercise C 3

- What can I do for you?
- We are making plans for our next holiday. We are looking for something extraordinary.
- Yes, something we've never done before.

Now go on. The following expressions will help you:

> spend some weeks in New York – climb Mount Everest – sail across the Atlantic Ocean – visit the Maoris in New Zealand – fly to Japan – cross the Sahara desert on the back of a camel – ~~be on safari in Africa~~

- Have you ever been on safari in Africa?
- Oh, yes we _____ often _____ there.
- And we _____ already _____

Past Tense und Present Perfect

Past Tense und Present Perfect   45

Fassen wir die letzten beiden Übungen noch einmal zusammen:

Have you ever been to Australia?

Oh, yes, we've been there before. Last year we spent three weeks there.

Regel

allgemeine Aussage
(Zeitpunkt nicht genannt)
often, never, ... ever ...? etc.　⟹　**Present Perfect**

zeitlich genau festgelegte
Handlung in der Vergangenheit
(Zeitpunkt genannt)　⟹　**Simple Past**
... ago, yesterday, last ... etc.

Have you ever been to England, Scotland, Wales or Ireland? And have you ever had a real "English breakfast" there?

Well, this is what a real English breakfast looks like:

English Breakfast

<u>Grapefruit or Juice</u> (Orange, Grapefruit, Tomato)

* * *

<u>Cereals</u>: Porridge, Cornflakes, All Bran, Rice Crispies

* * *

<u>Cooked Dishes</u>: Bacon or Sausages or Kippers[1],
　　　　　　　　Two Eggs (fried[2], boiled[3] or poached[4]),
　　　　　　Fried Bread or Toast, Baked Beans or Fried Tomato

* * *

<u>Toast, Breakfast Rolls or Croissants</u> with Butter, Marmalade, Jam
<u>Tea, Coffee, Milk</u>

---

1 geräucherter Hering
2 gebraten = Spiegelei
3 gekocht
4 pochiert = „verlorenes" Ei

By the way – English, Scottish, Welsh or Irish people don't have such a big breakfast every day! But for tourists it's a "must"!

Tobias is in England for the first time. After two days in London he and his classmates spend a fortnight[1] with English families. It's his first morning with the Stones in Wigan.

Exercise C 4

[1] 14 Tage

Mrs Stone: Have you ever had grapefruit juice before?
(have)

Tobias: have/often   Yes, I have often had it.

 buy/last week   My mother bought a bottle last week.

Mrs Stone: Have ....?
(eat)

Tobias: eat/last week   Yes, I .... it on the boat ....

Mrs Stone: ....?
(drink)

Tobias: drink/yet   No, I ....
 yesterday/have .... in London I .... coffee.

Mrs Stone: ....?
(taste)

Tobias: have/often   I .... them at home.

 try/never   But I .... them for breakfast. And I think they are different in Germany.

Mrs Stone: ....?
(eat)

Tobias: eat/never   Sugar puffs? No!
 I .... them before. But I would like to try them.

Past Tense und Present Perfect

C 2. Simple Past und Past Progressive
Simple past and past progressive

I was having a shower when the doorbell rang.

> Das **Past Progressive** hat einen länger andauernden Vorgang in der Vergangenheit zum Inhalt. Häufig beschreibt es eine Art **Hintergrundhandlung**, die gerade im Verlauf, d. h. noch nicht zu Ende war, als etwas Neues *(Simple Past!)* passierte.

Auf unserem Zeitstrahl würde das so aussehen:

when the doorbell rang

I was having a shower

Kannst du Fred helfen, die **Past Progressive-Formen** von *to have a shower* aufzuschreiben?

Exercise C 5

I was having a shower
you _____ a shower
he/she _____ a shower
we _____ a shower
you _____ a shower
they _____ a shower

What were they doing when it started to rain?

Exercise C 6

1. Tom and Judy ....
2. The Johnsons ....
3. Fred ....

4. Mr Greenfield ....
5. Linda, Joan and Kevin ....
6. Our neighbour's cat ....

In der folgenden Übung musst du entscheiden, wann du es mit einer Hintergrundhandlung und wann mit einer neu einsetzenden Handlung zu tun hast.

Simple Past or **Past Progressive**? Setze die richtige Verbform ein:

Exercise C 7

1. The pupils .... (throw) scraps[1] of paper at each other when the teacher .... (come) in.

1 Fetzen

2. While the Barristers .... (have) dinner, there .... (be) a knock at the door.
3. Sally .... (eat) a banana when a monkey suddenly .... (jump) on her shoulder.
4. The lights .... (go) out while we .... (play) cards.
5. While Sherlock Holmes, the famous detective, ... (look) at some pictures, he .... (have) an idea.
6. Fred .... (read) a ghost story when he suddenly .... (hear) footsteps.

Past Tense und Present Perfect

C 3. Der Gebrauch des *Present Perfect* mit *since* und *for*
The use of the present perfect with since and for

Poor Fred is seriously ill! He has got …

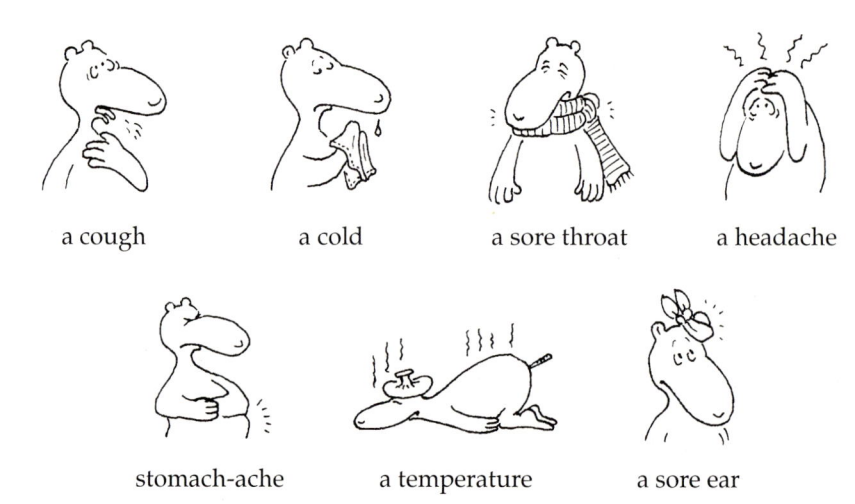

a cough   a cold   a sore throat   a headache

stomach-ache   a temperature   a sore ear

He has to see the doctor:

And how long have you had your cough?

I've had a sore throat for two days.

I've had it since yesterday.

> **!** Hier wird wieder deutlich, dass das englische **Present Perfect** eine Brücke zwischen Vergangenheit und Gegenwart schlägt: Freds Halsschmerzen fingen vor zwei Tagen an, und er hat sie jetzt immer noch.
> Im Deutschen verwendet man in diesem Fall das Präsens (die Gegenwart) – wie du siehst.

> Und wie lange hast du den Husten schon?

> Ich habe seit zwei Tagen Halsschmerzen.

> Den habe ich seit gestern.

Vielleicht ist dir noch etwas aufgefallen:

... *for* two days.   ... *seit* zwei Tagen
... *since* yesterday   ... *seit* gestern

Für das deutsche „seit" gibt es im Englischen zwei Übersetzungsmöglichkeiten:

for und *since*

Aber wann verwendet man nun das eine, wann das andere?

Das folgende Schaubild wird dir Klarheit verschaffen:

Fred has had a toothache ...

since Friday.

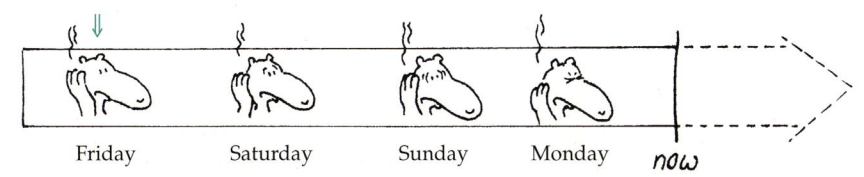

Friday   Saturday   Sunday   Monday   *now*

Beginn der Handlung

for four days.

Friday   Saturday   Sunday   Monday   *now*

Dauer der Handlung

Past Tense und Present Perfect

Regel

Wird der **Anfang** der Handlung genannt, steht im Englischen *since*:
since yesterday, since 3 o'clock, since 1989, since last Christmas.

Wird die **Dauer** der Handlung genannt, steht im Englischen *for*:
for two days, for a month, for three hours, for a while, for ages.

Exercise C 8

Nun antworte für Fred:

How long have you had …

… your headache? .... three days.

… your stomach-ache? .... two hours.

… a sore ear? .... last Tuesday.

… a sore throat? .... yesterday.

… your cold? .... two weeks.

Exercise C 9

Some personal questions: Answer with *since* or *for*.

How long have you had …

… this book? ....

… your bicycle? ....

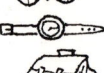

… your watch? ....

… your school bag? ....

… your cassette recorder? ....

And how long have you and your family had …

… your car? ....

… your flat or house? ....

… your dog, cat or other pet? ....

… your .... ? ....

… your .... ? ....

Past Tense und Present Perfect

Auch das *Present Perfect Progressive* steht häufig in Verbindung mit *since* oder *for*:

"I've been waiting for him since two o'clock!"

Kannst du Fred wieder helfen, die fehlenden Formen des *Present Perfect Progressive* zu ergänzen?

Exercise C 10

I have been waiting for him …

you ………………………………………………… for him …

he/she ……………………………………………… for him …

we ………………………………………………… for him …

you ………………………………………………… for him …

they ………………………………………………… for him …

Regel

Verwende das *Present Perfect Progressive*, wenn es sich um einen länger andauernden Vorgang handelt, der **in der Vergangenheit begonnen** hat und **in der Gegenwart noch andauert**.

Past Tense und Present Perfect

Exercise C 11   How long have they been doing it?

1. work in the garden/this morning

   Mr Brown has been working in the garden since this morning.

2. wash her car/five o'clock

   Carol

3. watch TV/half an hour

   Ann

4. read the newspaper/breakfast

   Tom's grandpa

5. write a letter/she came home from school

   Susan

6. prepare the dinner/two hours

   Mr Standish

7. suffer from stomach-ache/he ate that lovely cake

   Fred

8. play chess/three hours

   Tom and Peter

54   Past Tense und Present Perfect

Nachdem du die Verwendung von *Past Tense* und *Present Perfect* intensiv geübt hast, zum Abschluss unser Test:

Test

Übersetze ins Englische.
(Je 3 Punkte für jeden richtigen Satz. Punkteabzug bei Wortfehlern und falschen Verbformen)

Some tourists in London

1. Wir warten hier (schon) seit zwei Stunden!

2. Ich war noch nie im Tower von London – und jetzt ist er geschlossen!

3. Hast du diesen Hut gestern auf dem Portobello Market gekauft?

4. Wir gingen gerade zur Bushaltestelle, als es zu regnen anfing.

5. Ich habe diesen Schirm, seit ich im April letzten Jahres in London war.

6. Er steht seit 6 Uhr hier!

Testauswertung

My personal scoreboard:

18–14 "right" scores:
Excellent! Fred wouldn't have done better!

13–10 "right" scores:
Well done, indeed! If there is a tense you still have problems with – revise that part of the chapter. Then you won't have any difficulties in the future!

9–0 "right" scores:
Maybe you haven't read this chapter carefully enough. Do all the exercises – then you will be more successful!

Past Tense und Present Perfect

Hören und Sprechen

Eine gute englische Aussprache ist – wie so vieles – Trainingssache. Für ein Erfolg versprechendes Aussprachetraining brauchst du:
- einen Kassettenrekorder,
- eine besprochene Übungskassette (die es zu den meisten Lehrwerken und zu vielen Lektüren gibt),
- ein ruhiges Plätzchen und
- die Bereitschaft, gut zuzuhören.

1. Nachsprechübung

Höre dir einen Dialog oder Hörtext immer erst ganz an. Beim zweiten Durchgang drückst du nach jedem Satz oder Sinnabschnitt die Pausentaste und versuchst, das Gehörte möglichst genau nachzusprechen. Wenn dir ein Kassettenrekorder mit zwei Kassettenlaufwerken zur Verfügung steht, kannst du mit Hilfe der Aufnahme- und Pausentaste deine eigenen Äußerungen auf einer zweiten Kassette aufnehmen, später anhören und mit dem Original vergleichen.

2. Rollenspiel

In vielen Dialogen kommen typische Redewendungen vor, die man in einer bestimmten Situation verwendet (z. B. beim Einkaufen). Es ist äußerst sinnvoll, sich solche Ausdrücke besonders gut einzuprägen.
Dafür konzentrierst du dich auf eine Person in dem betreffenden Dialog. Sprich nur nach, was diese Person sagt, und wiederhole diese Nachsprechübung noch ein- bis zweimal. Dann übernimmst du die Rolle – das Drehbuch kennst du ja nun schon! Drücke die Pausentaste, bevor die bewusste Person zu Wort kommt, und sprich – wie ein Schauspieler – deinen Part.

3. Der kleine Unterschied

Achte beim Zuhören und Sprechen auch auf scheinbare Kleinigkeiten. Sie können mitunter ganz schön wichtig sein.

Bits & Pieces

Hörst du den Unterschied? Probiere selbst:

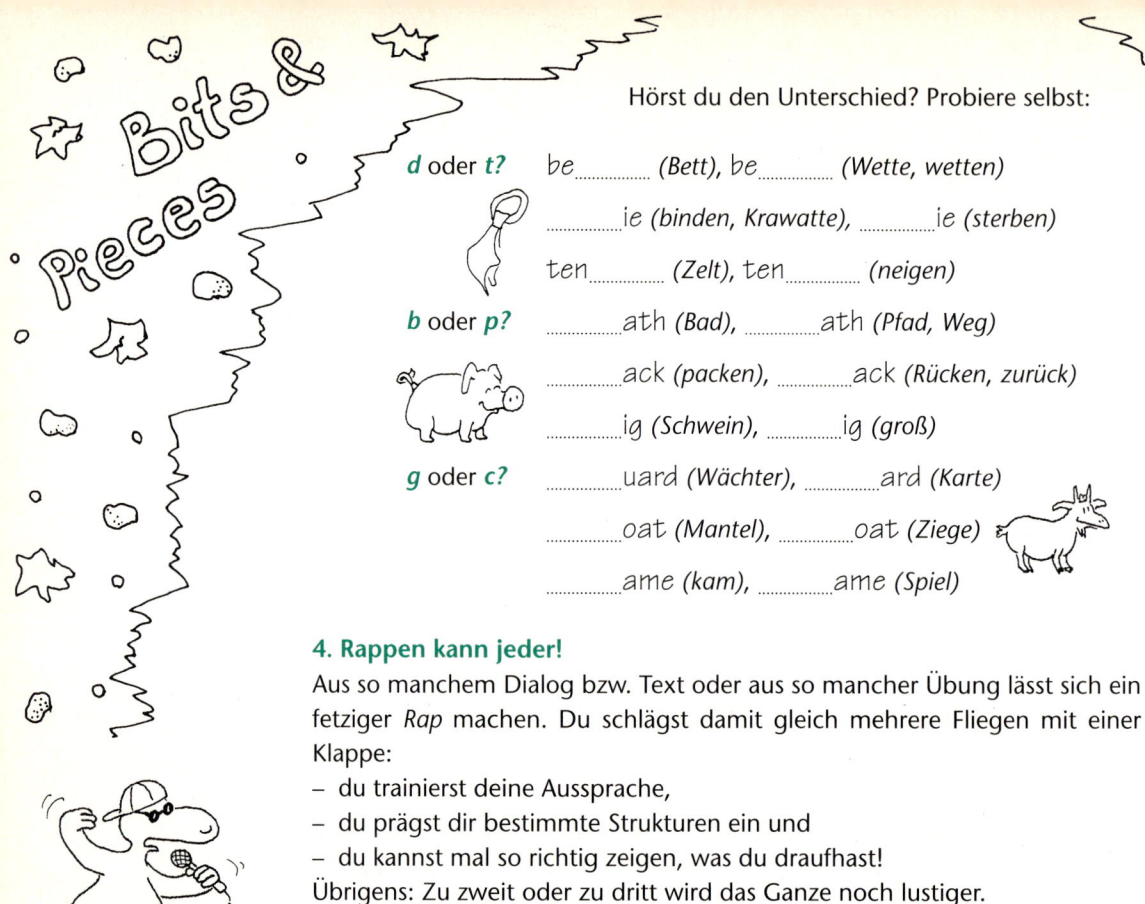

d oder t? be____ (Bett), be____ (Wette, wetten)
____ie (binden, Krawatte), ____ie (sterben)
ten____ (Zelt), ten____ (neigen)

b oder p? ____ath (Bad), ____ath (Pfad, Weg)
____ack (packen), ____ack (Rücken, zurück)
____ig (Schwein), ____ig (groß)

g oder c? ____uard (Wächter), ____ard (Karte)
____oat (Mantel), ____oat (Ziege)
____ame (kam), ____ame (Spiel)

4. Rappen kann jeder!

Aus so manchem Dialog bzw. Text oder aus so mancher Übung lässt sich ein fetziger *Rap* machen. Du schlägst damit gleich mehrere Fliegen mit einer Klappe:
– du trainierst deine Aussprache,
– du prägst dir bestimmte Strukturen ein und
– du kannst mal so richtig zeigen, was du draufhast!
Übrigens: Zu zweit oder zu dritt wird das Ganze noch lustiger.

Versuch's doch gleich mal mit einer Übung aus Kapitel B:
Du (oder ein Freund/eine Freundin) kannst als Begleitung rhythmisch mit dem Finger schnippen oder klatschen.

Do you understand me?	Yes, I do.
May I ask you some questions?	Yes, you may.
Are you from Mars?	No, I'm not.
Did you come by spacecraft?	No, I didn't.
Do your parents know where you are?	Yes, they do.
Would you like something to eat?	No, thank you.
Could you please tell me something about your planet?	Yes, of course.
Will you go back to your planet soon?	No, I won't. In fact, I'm going to a fancy-dress ball at my friend's house!

Halte Augen und Ohren offen – bestimmt findest du dann jede Menge Texte, die sich für einen *Rap* eignen!

Hören und Sprechen

Can, must, may – und ihre Ersatzformen
Can, must, may – and their substitutes

Ich konnte nicht früher kommen. Ich musste mein Fahrrad reparieren.

I couldn't come earlier. I had to repair my bike.

Können, müssen, dürfen – dieses Kapitel beschäftigt sich mit den englischen Varianten dieser Hilfsverben und ihren Ersatzformen.

Im Unterschied zum Deutschen können die modalen Hilfsverben *can*, *must* und *may* (können, müssen, dürfen) nicht alle Zeiten bilden. Deshalb heißen sie auch „unvollständige" Hilfsverben. Aber zum Glück gibt es Ersatzformen, die in allen Zeiten zum Einsatz kommen können! Apropos „können":

1. Das unvollständige Hilfsverb *can*
The defective auxiliary can

Tommy is now 18 months old.

He can | say "Mummy" and "Daddy".
       | walk without any help.
       | switch on the radio.
       | drink from a cup.
       | build a tower with his bricks.

You can also say: He is able to say "Mummy" and "Daddy".

Read the sentences aloud and use **is able to** instead of **can**.

Exercise D 1

können   can/be able to
(fähig sein, etwas zu tun)
Ich kann schwimmen.   I can swim. I'm able to swim.
Er kann schwimmen.   He can swim. He is able to swim.

Can, must, may   59

Last year Tommy was only six months old.

He **couldn't** say "Mummy" and "Daddy".
He **couldn't** …

Exercise D 2 Say what Tommy **couldn't** do when he was only six months old.

Instead of couldn't (could not) you can also say:

He **wasn't (was not) able to** say …
He **wasn't able to** …

Now say what Tommy **wasn't able to** do when he was only six months old.

Hier noch einmal das Hilfsverb „können" (fähig/in der Lage sein) im Überblick:

		Ersatzform:
ich kann schwimmen	*I can swim*	*I'm able to swim*
ich kann nicht schwimmen	*I cannot/can't swim*	*I'm not able to swim*
ich konnte schwimmen	*I could swim*	*I was able to swim*
ich konnte nicht schwimmen	*I could not/ couldn't swim*	*I was not able to swim I wasn't able to swim*

Can hat zwar eine Vergangenheitsform *(could)*, aber in allen anderen Zeiten musst du auf die Ersatzform *be able to* zurückgreifen. Dazu später mehr.

Neben der Bedeutung „fähig sein, etwas zu tun" hat *can* noch eine weitere:

„Kann ich mit Fred zum Schwimmen gehen?" Hier heißt „können" so viel wie „dürfen". Und in diesem Fall hat *can* dann auch eine andere Ersatzform: *be allowed to*.

Can, must, may

		Ersatzform:
können (fähig/in der Lage sein, etw. zu tun)	can	be able to
können (dürfen)	can	be allowed to

In der folgenden Übung geht es darum, die beiden Bedeutungen von *can* auseinander zu halten und die richtige Ersatzform zu verwenden.

Beispiel:
Wir konnten von unserem Hotelzimmer aus die Rocky Mountains sehen.

We *could / were able to* see the Rocky Mountains from our hotel room.

Exercise D 3

1. Meine Brieffreundin Fiona kann ein bisschen Deutsch sprechen.

   My penfriend Fiona _____ speak a little German.

2. Ich kann nicht mit zum Konzert gehen. Meine Eltern erlauben es nicht.

   I _____ go to the concert with you. …

3. Das Nilpferd konnte mit vier Bällen jonglieren.

   The hippo _____ juggle with four balls.

4. Simon hat seine Eltern gefragt – er kann mit uns zum Zelten fahren.

   … – he _____ go camping with us.

5. Auf den Autobahnen konnte man nicht mehr als 70 Meilen pro Stunde fahren.

   On the motorways you _____ drive more than 70 mph[1].   *1 Meilen pro Stunde*

Damit sind wir eigentlich schon beim nächsten unvollständigen Hilfsverb.

Can, must, may

D 2. Das unvollständige Hilfsverb *may*
The defective auxiliary *may*

Look at the following signs:

You *may* turn right, but you *may not* turn left or go straight ahead.
Wenn das Verbot – wie hier – sehr streng ist, kannst du auch sagen:
You *must not* turn left!

! Auch *may* ist ein unvollständiges Hilfsverb und kann keine Vergangenheit bilden. Die Ersatzform kennst du bereits:

You *are allowed to* turn right, but you *are not allowed to* turn left or to go straight ahead.

Exercise D 4

Write down what you may (not)/are (not) allowed to do when you see the following signs:

1. You ……*may*…… / ……*are allowed to*…… use this door only in case of emergency.

2. You ………………………… enter the road.

3. You ………………………… overtake cars, but you ………………………… overtake tractors.

4. You ………………………… bring your dog to the zoo, but you must keep it on the lead.

5. You ………………………… smoke here.

Can, must, may

Hier die Gegenwarts- und Vergangenheitsformen von *may* im Überblick:

		Ersatzform:
ich darf gehen ich darf nicht gehen	*I may go* *I may not go* *(I mustn't go)*	*I am/I'm allowed to go* *I am/I'm not allowed to go*
ich durfte gehen ich durfte nicht gehen	– –	*I was allowed to go* *I was not/wasn't allowed to go*

In der folgenden Übung erzählt Fred von seiner ersten Klassenfahrt:

What were Fred and his classmates allowed/not allowed to do?

We .... listen to music in our rooms or play cards in the evenings, but not longer than ten o'clock.

We .... make any noise after ten.

Exercise D 5

There was a little lake nearby, but

I .... go swimming there! We

.... go to the public swimming-bath – well, better than nothing!

They had quite a number of bicycles and go-carts, and we ....

.... use them whenever we wanted. That was great fun!
On the last day my friend Chris wanted to go shopping to the town centre.

He .... to go alone, so I went with him.

Can, must, may

D 3. Das unvollständige Hilfsverb *must*
The defective auxiliary must

I'm terribly sorry, Fred, I can't play table-tennis with you this afternoon.

Why not?

Well, I must help Grandma this afternoon. She's in bed with flu. First I must do the shopping for her. Then I must fetch her some medicine from the chemist's. After that I must make her some tea. And then I must feed Tiffy, her cat. When I come home I must do my homework. And then it will be too late.

Well, I hope your grandmother is better soon. If you like – I could help you with the shopping and all that!

Instead of *must* you can use its substitute *have to*:

Read Ann's answer aloud and use *have to*:

Well,
I **have to** help Granny this afternoon. …

Exercise D 6   First I **have to** …

Exercise D 7   This is what Fred tells his mother after he has talked to Ann on the phone:

We can't play table-tennis today, because Ann's grandma is ill. Ann **has to** help her this afternoon. She **has to** …

"Go on!"

Exercise D 8   In the evening Ann writes into her diary:

After school I couldn't play table-tennis with Fred. I **had to** help Granny all afternoon. But Fred came with me and gave me a hand. That was really nice of him! First we **had to** …
…
When I came home I …

"Go on!"

Can, must, may

Na, das klappt ja bestens! Es fehlt jetzt eigentlich nur noch die verneinte Form „etwas nicht tun müssen", dann birgt auch dieses unvollständige Hilfsverb keine Rätsel mehr. Aber jetzt heißt es:

Aufgepasst!

nicht müssen ≠ mustn't

Erinnerst du dich, in welchem Zusammenhang *mustn't* in diesem Kapitel schon einmal aufgetaucht ist? Genau – in Verbindung mit dem unvollständigen Hilfsverb *may*:

You *may not* turn left or go straight on.
You *mustn't* turn left or go straight on!

mustn't = nicht dürfen

Und wie drückt man nun im Englischen aus, wenn jemand etwas nicht tun muss?

In der folgenden Übersicht sind die wichtigsten Formen zusammengefasst:

		Ersatzform:
ich muss gehen	*I must go*	*I have to go*
er muss gehen	*he must go*	*he has to go*
ich muss nicht gehen	*I needn't go*	*I don't have to go*
er muss nicht gehen	*he needn't go*	*he doesn't have to go*
ich musste gehen	–	*I had to go*
er musste gehen	–	*he had to go*
ich musste nicht gehen	–	*I didn't have to go*
er musste nicht gehen	–	*he didn't have to go*

Can, must, may

Exercise D 9

In den Ferien muss man viele Dinge **nicht** tun, die sonst den Tagesablauf bestimmen. In der nächsten Übung träumt Nick gerade davon, was er in den Ferien nicht tun muss.

Holidays are great!

- not go to bed at eight
- not write any tests
- not get up at half past six
- not do any homework in the afternoon
- not wear my school uniform
- not hurry to catch the bus

Nick thinks: In the holidays …

I **don't have to** get up half past six.
I **don't have to** …
…

"Go on!"

You could also say:

I **needn't** get up at half past six.
I **needn't** …
…

"Go on!"

Now say what Nick **doesn't have to do** in the holidays:

He **doesn't have to** get up at half past six.
He **doesn't have to** …

"Go on!"

66 Can, must, may

Damit du *mustn't* und *needn't (don't/doesn't have to)* nicht so leicht verwechselst, hier noch eine Übung:

Don't forget:

You needn't do that.   Du brauchst das nicht tun.
You don't have to do that.   Du musst das nicht tun.
You mustn't do that!   Du darfst das nicht tun!

Exercise D 10

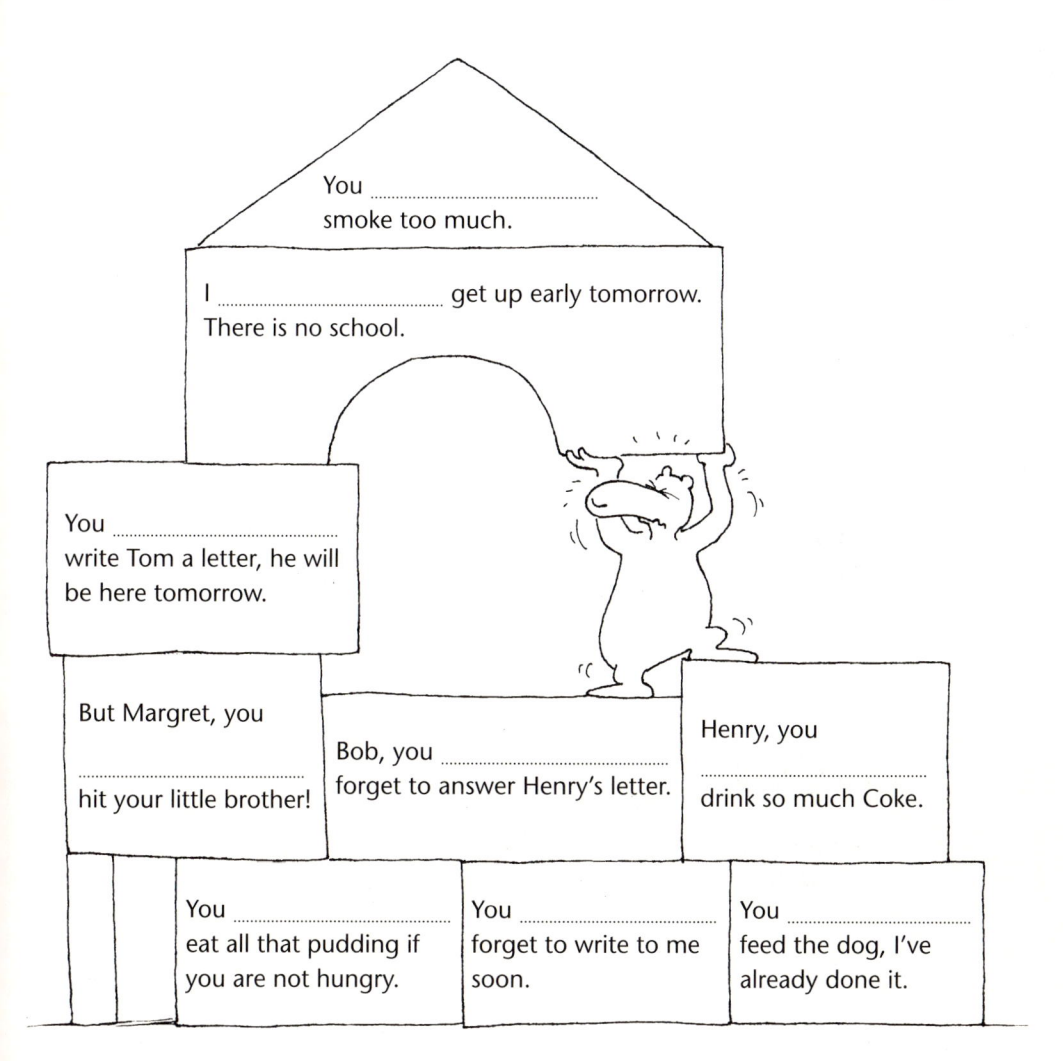

You .... smoke too much.

I .... get up early tomorrow. There is no school.

You .... write Tom a letter, he will be here tomorrow.

But Margret, you .... hit your little brother!

Bob, you .... forget to answer Henry's letter.

Henry, you .... drink so much Coke.

You .... eat all that pudding if you are not hungry.

You .... forget to write to me soon.

You .... feed the dog, I've already done it.

You can colour the bricks if you like:

– use **red** for the bricks with *mustn't*,
– **yellow** for the bricks with *needn't/don't have to*

Can, must, may 67

Exercise D 11

In vielen Familien gibt es häufig unerfreuliche Debatten, z. B. über die Frage, wer heute wieder den Hund ausführen oder wer das Geschirr abräumen soll. Kommt dir das irgendwie bekannt vor? Familie Sullivan hat dieses Problem auf ihre Weise gelöst: Für jede Woche gibt es einen „Dienstplan", in dem vermerkt ist, welche Aufgaben von welchem Familienmitglied zu erledigen sind:

	Mon	Tue	Wed	Thu	Fri	Sat	Sun
feed the rabbits + clean their cages	Paul	Paul	Paul	Paul	Paul	Paul	Paul
go for a walk with Scruffy (the dog)	Mum	Chris	Chris	Dad	Chris	Dad	Angie
water the flowers	Angie		Angie		Angie		Angie
lay the table	Dad + Chris						
clear the table	Angie + Paul						

Now say what Angie, Chris, Paul, Mr and Mrs Sullivan *had to do/didn't have to do* last week:

Example:

Last week Angie **had to** ...
She **didn't have to** ...
...

Chris **had to** ... on Tuesday, Wednesday and Friday
he **didn't have to** ...
Dad and Chris ...
...

Say what **you** had to do yesterday/last week!

Can, must, may

Zum Abschluss kannst du jetzt überprüfen, ob du mit allen unvollständigen Hilfsverben bzw. ihren Ersatzformen zurechtkommst.

At the zoo

Exercise D 12

There is a small zoo in our town. Last week I _____ (durfte) go there with my sister. My father _____ (konnte nicht) come with us, he _____ (musste) work, so we _____ (mussten) _____ take the bus. I _____ (durfte) take my brother's camera with me but I _____ (musste) promise him to be very careful.

When we reached the entrance we first _____ (mussten) buy the tickets. My sister _____ (durfte) visit the zoo for half the price, as she is only eight years old. First we went to the monkeys. There was a sign: You _____ (dürfen nicht) feed the animals. The keeper told us that people who fed the monkeys _____ (mussten) _____ pay a high fine[1].

1 Geldstrafe

My sister likes the hippopotamus very much. She was very happy when she _____ (durfte) help the keeper to feed it. I _____ (musste) _____ take a picture of her in front of the pool. We _____ (durften) ride on the elephant that carries visitors through the zoo. At six o'clock we _____ (mussten) leave the zoo.

Can, must, may

D 4. Die unvollständigen Hilfsverben *can, must, may* und die Zukunft
The defective auxiliaries *can, must, may* and the Future

> Do you think the kids on Earth will be able to understand us?

> Yes, of course. They learn Xenophonic at school. But we will have to speak slowly.

> I hope we will be allowed to send messages home via satellite. I've never been away from Xenos for such a long time!

So könnte Schüleraustausch im Jahr 2222 aussehen: Die beiden Jugendlichen vom Planeten Xenos befinden sich an Bord eines Raumschiffes, das eine Schülergruppe zur Erde bringt. Dort werden sie zwei Jahre lang zur Schule gehen und in Familien leben.

Die Zukunftsformen von *can*, *must* und *may* beherrschen die beiden Xenosianer schon recht gut. Und du?

Exercise D 13

Ergänze die fehlenden Formen. Tipp: Schau dir die Sprechblasen noch einmal genau an!

Present		Future
they **can** understand	they **are able to** understand	they .... understand
they **can't** understand	they **are not able to** understand	they **will not (won't) be able to** understand
we **must** speak	we **have to** speak	we ....
we **needn't** speak	we **don't have to** ...	we ....
I **may** send	I **am allowed to** ...	I ....
I **may not/ mustn't** send	I **am not allowed to** ...	I ....

70 *Can, must, may*

Xsi ist ein bisschen aufgeregt und macht sich viele Gedanken über den bevorstehenden Aufenthalt auf der Erde. Xias Vater war schon einmal als Austauschlehrer auf der Erde, und sie kann daher Xsis Fragen beantworten:

Fill in the **future tense forms**.

Exercise D 14

1. .... we .... (can) see Xenos from there?

2. No, you .... (cannot) see Xenos – it's too far away and it's too small. But there will be a video call every ten days, and you .... (can) see and talk to your family then.

3. Do you think we .... (must) stay inside the buildings all the time?

4. No, not at all. Earth kids like playing outside. When it rains or snows, we .... (must) wear special clothes.

5. .... we .... (must) go to school every day?

6. No. We .... (need not) go to school at the weekends, that is on Saturday and Sunday.

7. Is it true that we .... (may not) speak Xenophonic¹ at school?

8. That's right. We .... (must) speak Earthian² at school. But we .... (may) meet once a week and speak our own language then.

1 Xenophonic – hier: ausländisch, Sprache des Planeten Xenos
2 Earthian – hier: Sprache der Erdbewohner
3 Erdanziehung

9. I've heard that they have a game called "baseball" on Earth. I hope I .... (can) play it – with all that gravitation³ on Earth!

10. I'm sure you .... (may) join the school baseball team. And you will get used to gravitation within a short time.

Can, must, may

Test

Translate the following sentences:
Manchmal gibt es zwei Möglichkeiten, das Hilfsverb zu übersetzen.
(Je 2 Punkte für jeden richtigen Satz)

1. Als ich Windpocken hatte, durfte ich eine Woche lang nicht in die Schule gehen.

   When I had chickenpox, ...

   ....

2. Nächstes Jahr wird mein Bruder schwimmen können.

   ....

3. Ihr braucht/müsst nicht auf mich warten.

   ....

4. Ich konnte mit sechs Jahren noch nicht Fahrrad fahren.

   ....

5. Mr Brown wird zwei Stunden warten müssen. Der nächste Zug fährt um 10.20 Uhr.

   ....

   ....

   The next train leaves at 10.20 a. m.

1 employees

6. In vielen Büros dürfen die Angestellten[1] nicht rauchen.

   ....

   ....

7. Jack muss heute auf seinen kleinen Bruder aufpassen.

   ....

8. Susan wird morgen nicht Volleyball spielen können. Sie hat sich den Knöchel verstaucht.

   ....

   ....

   She has sprained her ankle.

72 Can, must, may

Testauswertung

My personal scoreboard:

16–12 "right" scores:
This is an excellent result. You can be proud of yourself!

11–8 "right" scores:
Not bad! Analyse your mistakes and revise the forms you have problems with. Then you will soon be an expert in this field!

7–0 "right" scores:
You **can** do better than that! Are you sure you did **all** the exercises in this chapter? Well, then – work your way through this chapter again!

Can, must, may

Bits & Pieces

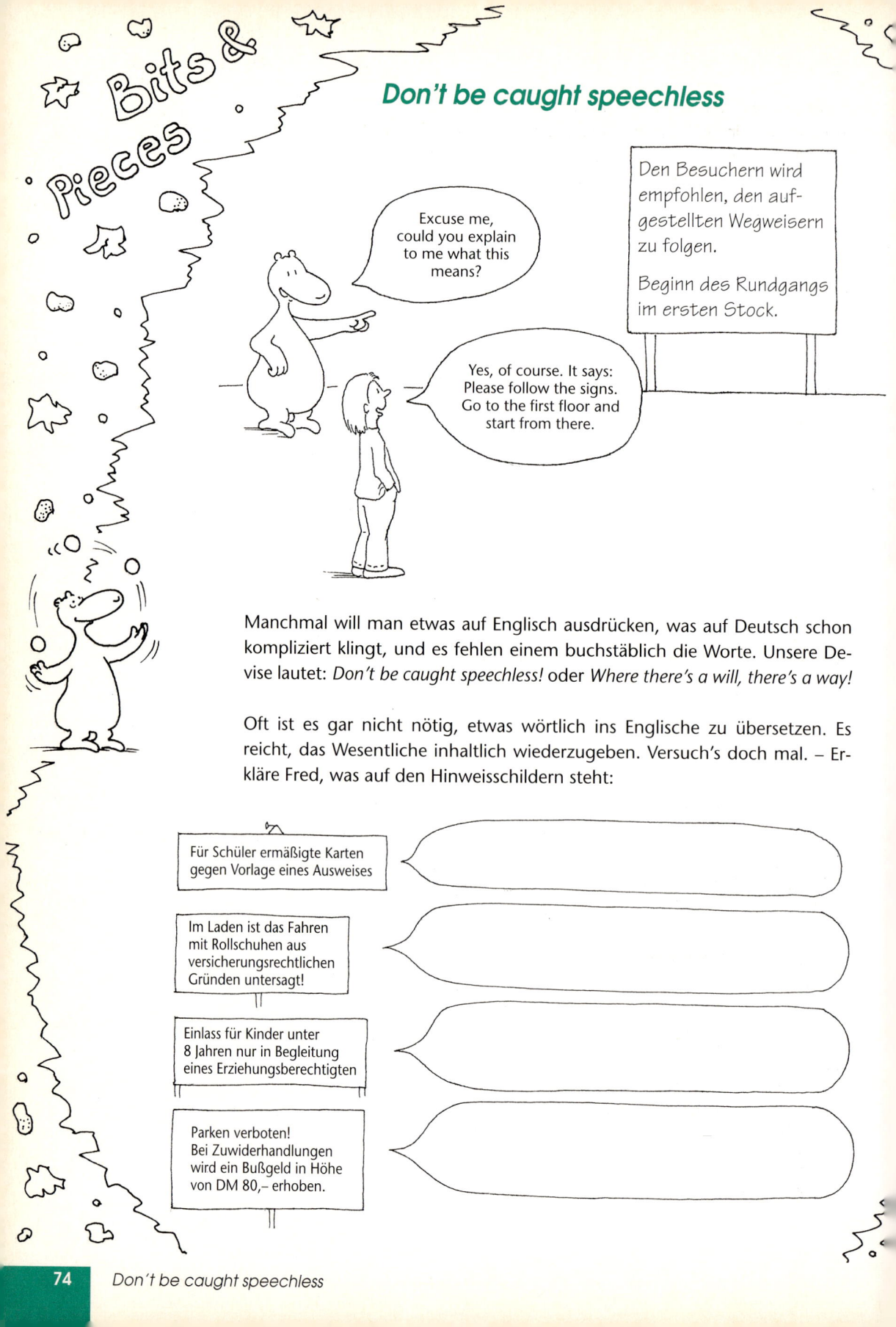

Don't be caught speechless

Excuse me, could you explain to me what this means?

Yes, of course. It says: Please follow the signs. Go to the first floor and start from there.

Den Besuchern wird empfohlen, den aufgestellten Wegweisern zu folgen.

Beginn des Rundgangs im ersten Stock.

Manchmal will man etwas auf Englisch ausdrücken, was auf Deutsch schon kompliziert klingt, und es fehlen einem buchstäblich die Worte. Unsere Devise lautet: *Don't be caught speechless!* oder *Where there's a will, there's a way!*

Oft ist es gar nicht nötig, etwas wörtlich ins Englische zu übersetzen. Es reicht, das Wesentliche inhaltlich wiederzugeben. Versuch's doch mal. – Erkläre Fred, was auf den Hinweisschildern steht:

Für Schüler ermäßigte Karten gegen Vorlage eines Ausweises

Im Laden ist das Fahren mit Rollschuhen aus versicherungsrechtlichen Gründen untersagt!

Einlass für Kinder unter 8 Jahren nur in Begleitung eines Erziehungsberechtigten

Parken verboten! Bei Zuwiderhandlungen wird ein Bußgeld in Höhe von DM 80,– erhoben.

Don't be caught speechless

Manchmal fehlt dir in einer Unterhaltung oder beim Schreiben vielleicht nur ein bestimmtes Wort. Du willst es aber nicht einfach übergehen, weil es für deine Geschichte wichtig ist. Auch hier heißt es: flexibel sein! Du kannst das betreffende Wort so um- oder beschreiben, dass dein Gesprächspartner leicht darauf kommt, was du meinst.

So I took a …?

It's a tool. You need it if you want to take something apart.

Now it's your turn! Explain or describe the following things:

Schnorchel

Büroklammer

Spaten

Seestern

Kaulquappen

Schubkarre

Satellitenschüssel

Stabhochsprung

Don't be caught speechless

Indirekte Rede: Aussagesätze
Reported speech: statements

Hier lernst du, wie man das wiedergibt, was eine andere Person gesagt hat.

1 Still! Pst!

The Smiths are watching their favourite series on TV:

In diesen Szenen eines Fernsehabends wird einiges gesprochen – sowohl auf dem Bildschirm als auch im Wohnzimmer der Smiths. In einer der Szenen wird das wiedergegeben, was eine andere Person vorher gesagt hat. Erinnerst du dich, welches Bild gemeint ist? – Granny hat wohl den Dialog zwischen Winston und Laura nicht ganz verstanden. In Bild 4 berichtet ihr Enkel, was genau gesagt wurde. Das bezeichnet man als **indirekte Rede** (*Reported Speech*).

In einem Roman wäre die Szene vielleicht so zu lesen:

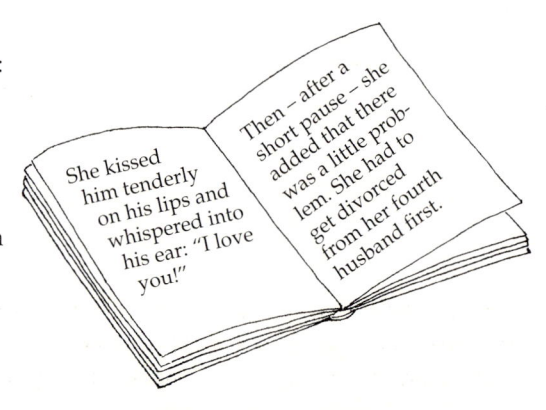

Die wörtliche Rede – das, was die einzelnen Personen sagen – ist in Anführungszeichen gesetzt. In der indirekten Rede fallen diese Anführungszeichen weg.

76 Indirekte Rede: Aussagesätze

Lies die folgenden Sätze genau durch und trage sie in die richtige Spalte der Tabelle ein:

Oma sagte: „Ich habe mein Hörgerät verloren."
Granny said she had lost her hearing aid.
Granny said: "I've lost my hearing aid."
Oma sagt, sie habe ihr Hörgerät verloren.

Exercise E 1

	Direct Speech Wörtliche Rede	*Reported Speech* Indirekte Rede
englischer Satz		
deutscher Satz		

Bestimmt ist dir aufgefallen, dass in der **indirekten Rede** im Englischen **das Verb in einer anderen Zeit** steht als in der direkten Rede. Das liegt daran, dass das **einleitende Verb** (*Granny said …*) im *Past Tense* steht.

Whenever Mrs Jennings asks her daughter Helen to help her with the housework, Helen says that she has to do a lot of homework.

(Sprechblase: But I have to do a lot of homework!)

Steht das einleitende Verb in der Gegenwart, ändert sich die Zeit in der indirekten Rede **nicht**. Da diese Fälle meist keine Schwierigkeiten bereiten, wollen wir uns hier nicht weiter mit ihnen beschäftigen.

Aber auch die Veränderung der Zeiten in den Sätzen, in denen das einleitende Verb in der Vergangenheit steht, ist eigentlich ganz einfach. Es gibt dafür feste Regeln. Wenn du sie beachtest, kannst du kaum etwas falsch machen.

Indirekte Rede: Aussagesätze

E 1. Die Zeitenfolge in der indirekten Rede
The change of tenses in indirect speech

This is what the presidential candidate said in his speech:

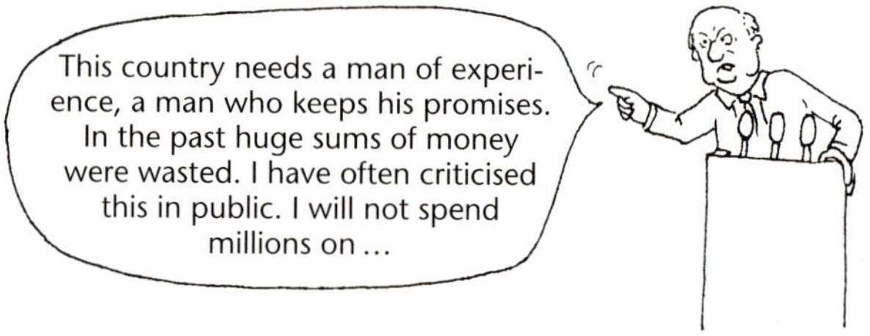

> This country needs a man of experience, a man who keeps his promises. In the past huge sums of money were wasted. I have often criticised this in public. I will not spend millions on …

> In his speech at a party meeting last night the Republican candidate said that this country needed a man of experience, a man who kept his promises. He went on to say that in the past huge sums of money had been wasted, and that he had often criticised that in public. He told his audience that he would not spend millions on …

Ergänze das folgende Schaubild. Dann wirst du ganz leicht erkennen, wie sich die Zeiten in der indirekten Rede verändern.

Exercise E 2

	Direct Speech	Reported Speech
Verb	needs	needed
Tense	Simple Present	Simple Past
Verb	keeps	
Tense	....	....
Verb	were wasted	
Tense	Simple Past	....
Verb	have criticised	
Tense	Present Perfect	....

An einem Zeitstrahl lässt sich die Zeitverschiebung gut darstellen:

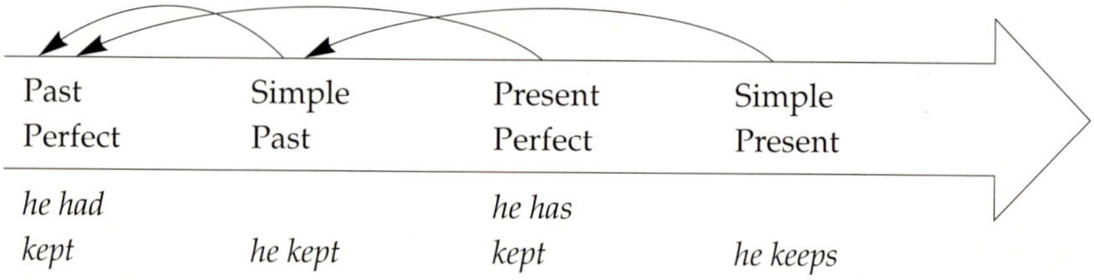

Past Perfect	Simple Past	Present Perfect	Simple Present
he had kept	*he kept*	*he has kept*	*he keeps*

Indirekte Rede: Aussagesätze

Bei der Umwandlung von der wörtlichen Rede in die indirekte Rede überspringen die Verben jeweils eine Zeitstufe nach hinten. Lediglich vom *Simple Past* zum *Past Perfect* ist nur ein kleinerer Sprung möglich. Und beim *Past Perfect* ist Endstation: *Past Perfect* in der wörtlichen Rede bleibt auch in der indirekten Rede *Past Perfect*.

Diese Zeitenfolge gilt übrigens auch für die jeweiligen Verlaufsformen (*Progressive Forms*):

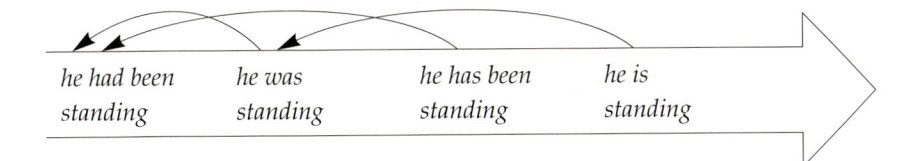

he had been standing — *he was standing* — *he has been standing* — *he is standing*

Hier noch einmal die Regel:

> Steht das **einleitende Verb** in der **Vergangenheit**, ändert sich die Zeit bei der Umwandlung von wörtlicher in indirekte Rede wie folgt:
>
> Present Tense ⟶ Past Tense
> Present Perfect ⟶ Past Perfect
> Past Tense ⟶ Past Perfect
> Past Perfect bleibt Past Perfect

Regel

Und was wird aus dem Futur?

Schauen wir uns noch einmal den letzten Satz der Rede an, die der ehrgeizige Präsidentschaftskandidat gehalten hat.

Er sagte: *"I will not spend millions on ..."*

Aus dem Munde der Nachrichtensprecherin klang das so:

He said that he would not spend millions on ...

Ergänzen wir also die oben aufgeführte Regel:

> Future I ⟶ Conditional I
> (will + Verb)   (would + Verb)

Regel

Indirekte Rede: Aussagesätze

Exercise E 3

Now it's your turn!

Bad luck

John wanted to go to Sarah's birthday party, but he's in hospital now. His mother rings up Sarah and tells her what happened:

John is very sorry that he can't come to your party. He has been taken to hospital. There was a football match at the school this morning. It was the final of the school championship. John was just running to get the ball when he slipped, fell and broke his ankle. Fortunately, his leg doesn't hurt too badly. He will stay in hospital for two days and he won't be able to go to school for at least a week.

In the afternoon Sarah tells her friends:

John's mother rang me up an hour ago. She said he ____was____

very sorry that he _____ to the party. She told me

(that) he _____ to hospital. There _____

a football match at the school this morning. It _____

the final of the school championship. She said (that) John _____

_____ to get the ball when he _____

_____ his ankle. Fortunately, his leg _____

_____ too badly. She also said he _____ in

hospital for two days and he _____ to go to school
for at least a week.

In einigen Sätzen der vorangegangen Übung war ein Wort eingeklammert, das man einfügen oder auch weglassen kann: *that* (dass).

His mother told me that he had been taken to hospital.
  Seine Mutter sagte mir, dass er ins Krankenhaus gebracht worden sei.

His mother told me he had been taken to hospital.
  Seine Mutter sagte mir, er sei ins Krankenhaus gebracht worden.

Du kannst von Fall zu Fall entscheiden, ob du die Version mit oder ohne *that* bevorzugst.

Indirekte Rede: Aussagesätze

Das kannst du gleich in der nächsten Übung ausprobieren.

The Bush Fire

Sandy Smith liest ihrer Großmutter oft aus Büchern vor. Da ihre Oma schwerhörig ist, muss Sandy manchmal einzelne Sätze wiederholen. Sie verwendet dabei die indirekte Rede.

Exercise E 4

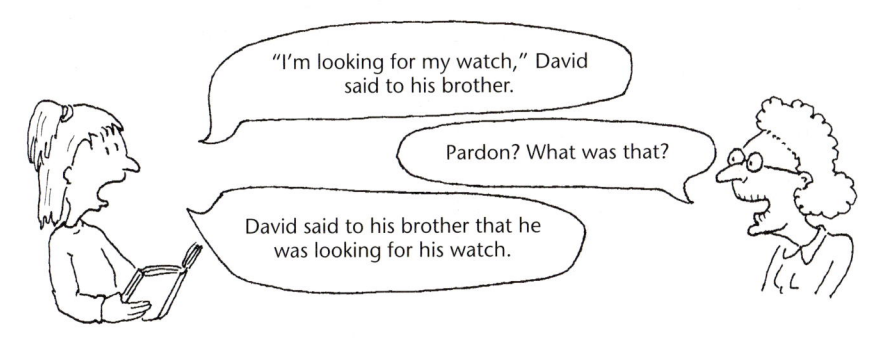

"I'm looking for my watch," David said to his brother.

Pardon? What was that?

David said to his brother that he was looking for his watch.

Wiederhole nun auch die folgenden Sätze in indirekter Rede:

1. He said: "I had a fight with a kangaroo."

   ....

2. David told Steve: "The birds are flying north."

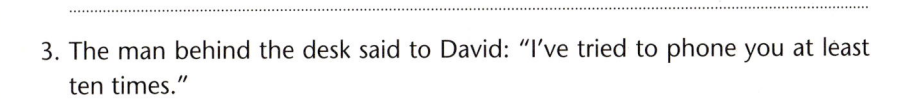

   ....

3. The man behind the desk said to David: "I've tried to phone you at least ten times."

   ....

   ....

4. Helen said: "I'm sure that the two men will be found."

   ....

   ....

5. Jim said to the fireman: "I need a helmet and an axe."

   ....

6. He added: "Something has to be done!"

   ....

7. The reporter said: "Nobody was killed in the fire."

   ....

Indirekte Rede: Aussagesätze

E 2. Weitere Veränderungen in der indirekten Rede
More changes in indirect speech

Häufig verändert sich in der indirekten Rede nicht nur die Zeitform des Verbs.

> We will leave for Eurodisney tomorrow!

> Tina said they would leave for Eurodisney tomorrow.

> On Friday Tina told me they would leave for Eurodisney the next day.

Friday, 10 a.m.   *Friday, 6 p.m.*   *Sunday, 3 p.m.*

Du siehst, auch Pronomen und Zeitangaben werden verändert. Und zwar so:

! we ⟶ they
tomorrow ⟶ the next day

Die **Veränderung** ist **abhängig** davon, **von wem**, **wo** und **wann** das **Gesagte wiedergegeben** wird.

Hier eine Liste der häufigsten Veränderungen:

Wortliste Zeitangaben

today	that day
tonight	that night
this morning/afternoon	that morning/afternoon
yesterday	the day before
	the previous day
tomorrow	the next day
	the following day
now	then, at that point
next week/month/year	the following week/month/year
last week	the previous week
	the week before
an hour/a week ago	an hour/a week before

Ortsangaben

here	there, in that place
in this street	in that street

Indirekte Rede: Aussagesätze

Alles klar? Dann versuch's mal mit der folgenden Übung:

Paul's friend Tony and his family have moved to another town. One day Paul visits them there. This is what Tony tells him:

① There are no kids in our neighbourhood here.

② My new school is more than five miles away.

③ My new classmates are really nice. Some of them asked me to join the football team.

④ Tomorrow I'm going to a school party.

⑤ Yesterday I was at the sports centre. It's great! I've never seen anything like this before!

Exercise E 5

A few days later Paul tells his friends at home:

1. Last week I visited Tony and his family. Tony said ....

2. He explained to me that ....

3. And he said ....

4. Then he told me ....

5. He also told me ....

Bist du noch fit für den Test? Na, dann los!

Indirekte Rede: Aussagesätze 83

Test

(Je 1 Punkt für jede Verbform und für jeden Ausdruck, der sich in der indirekten Rede verändert)

Europe in seven days

Mr Running from San Francisco is "doing" Europe in seven days. From Paris he rings up his wife. Here is what he tells her:

"I'm ringing you up from Paris. It's a beautiful city. I've already seen the Eiffel Tower. Yesterday we went to Versailles, that famous castle where the French kings had lived. There is gold everywhere, but I didn't see any bathrooms! Before that we had been to the Rhine Valley. We have to get up very early. Yes, I'm a little tired today and I don't feel like going to the opera tonight! I don't have much time for writing postcards, either. Tomorrow I will be in Rome. A bus will take us to the most interesting sights. I've already taken hundreds of photos. Well, I have to go now! We are going to the Louvre …"

Two days later Mrs Running meets her neighbour. She tells her about the phone call:

"Yes, he called me the day before yesterday. He said he _____ from Paris and it _____ a beautiful city. He told me that he _____ the Eiffel Tower. _____ they _____ to Versailles, that famous castle where the French kings _____. Rupert said that there _____ gold everywhere, but he _____ any bathrooms! Before that _____ to the Rhine Valley. He told me that _____ very early and that he _____ a little tired _____. He _____ like going to the opera _____! He also said he _____ much time for writing postcards. He then explained to me that _____ in Rome _____. A bus _____ to the most interesting sights. The last thing he said was that he _____ hundreds of photos and that he _____ to go _____ because they _____ to the Louvre."

Indirekte Rede: Aussagesätze

Testauswertung

My personal scoreboard:

22–17 "right" scores:
Excellent! You couldn't have done better!

16–11 "right" scores:
That's really good for a start! You just need a little more practice. Revise the tenses (chapter A in this book) or the aspects of the reported speech you had problems with.

10–0 "right" scores:
Are you sure you read the whole chapter and did all the exercises? You will see: practice makes perfect!

Indirekte Rede: Aussagesätze

How to use the dictionary

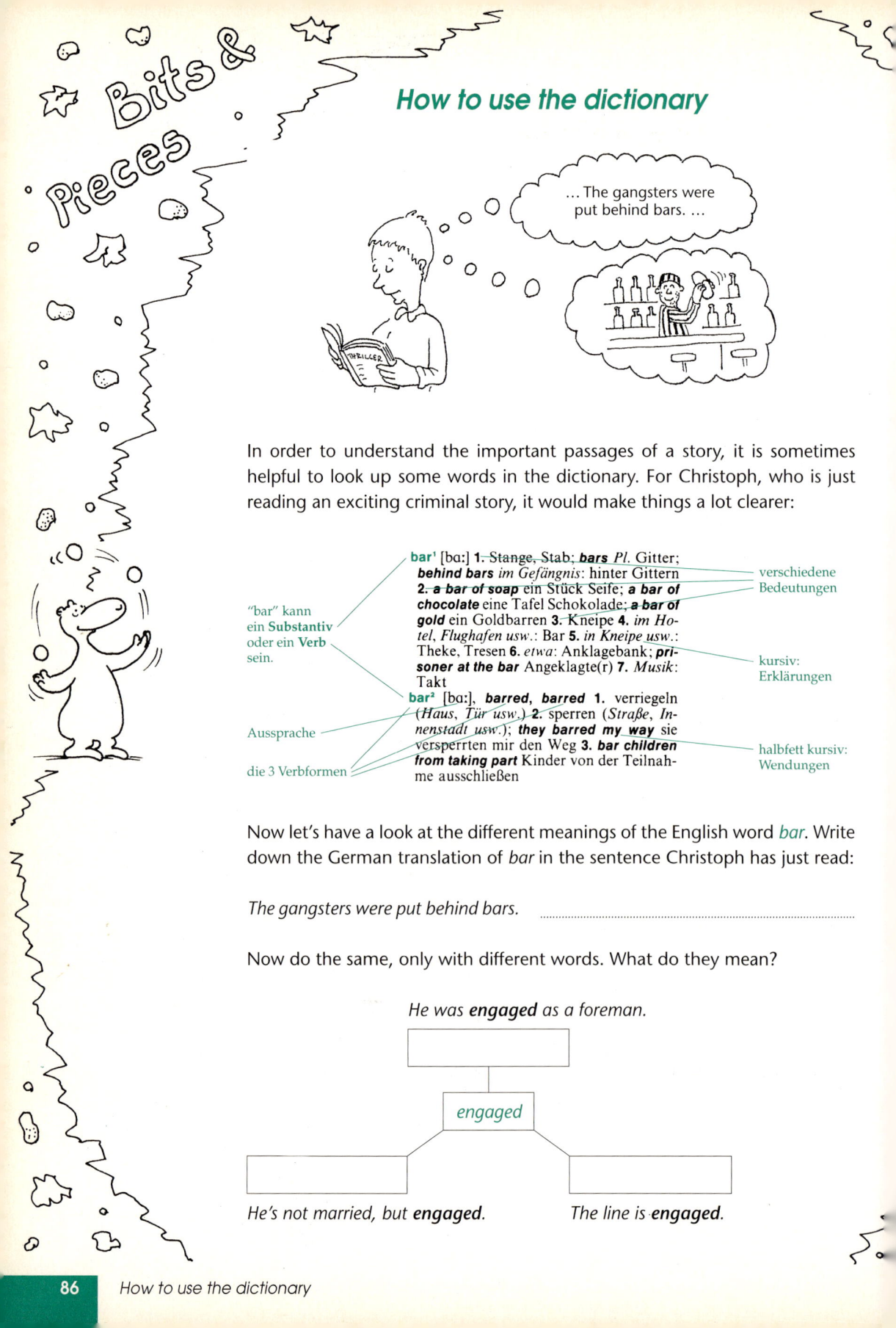

... The gangsters were put behind bars. ...

In order to understand the important passages of a story, it is sometimes helpful to look up some words in the dictionary. For Christoph, who is just reading an exciting criminal story, it would make things a lot clearer:

"bar" kann ein **Substantiv** oder ein **Verb** sein.

Aussprache

die 3 Verbformen

bar¹ [bɑː] **1.** Stange, Stab; **bars** *Pl.* Gitter; **behind bars** *im Gefängnis:* hinter Gittern **2. a bar of soap** ein Stück Seife; **a bar of chocolate** eine Tafel Schokolade; **a bar of gold** ein Goldbarren **3.** Kneipe **4.** *im Hotel, Flughafen usw.:* Bar **5.** *in Kneipe usw.:* Theke, Tresen **6.** *etwa:* Anklagebank; **prisoner at the bar** Angeklagte(r) **7.** *Musik:* Takt
bar² [bɑː], **barred**, **barred 1.** verriegeln (*Haus, Tür usw.*) **2.** sperren (*Straße, Innenstadt usw.*); **they barred my way** sie versperrten mir den Weg **3. bar children from taking part** Kinder von der Teilnahme ausschließen

verschiedene Bedeutungen

kursiv: Erklärungen

halbfett kursiv: Wendungen

Now let's have a look at the different meanings of the English word *bar*. Write down the German translation of *bar* in the sentence Christoph has just read:

The gangsters were put behind bars. ....

Now do the same, only with different words. What do they mean?

He was **engaged** as a foreman.

engaged

He's not married, but **engaged**.   The line is **engaged**.

86 How to use the dictionary

Bits & Pieces

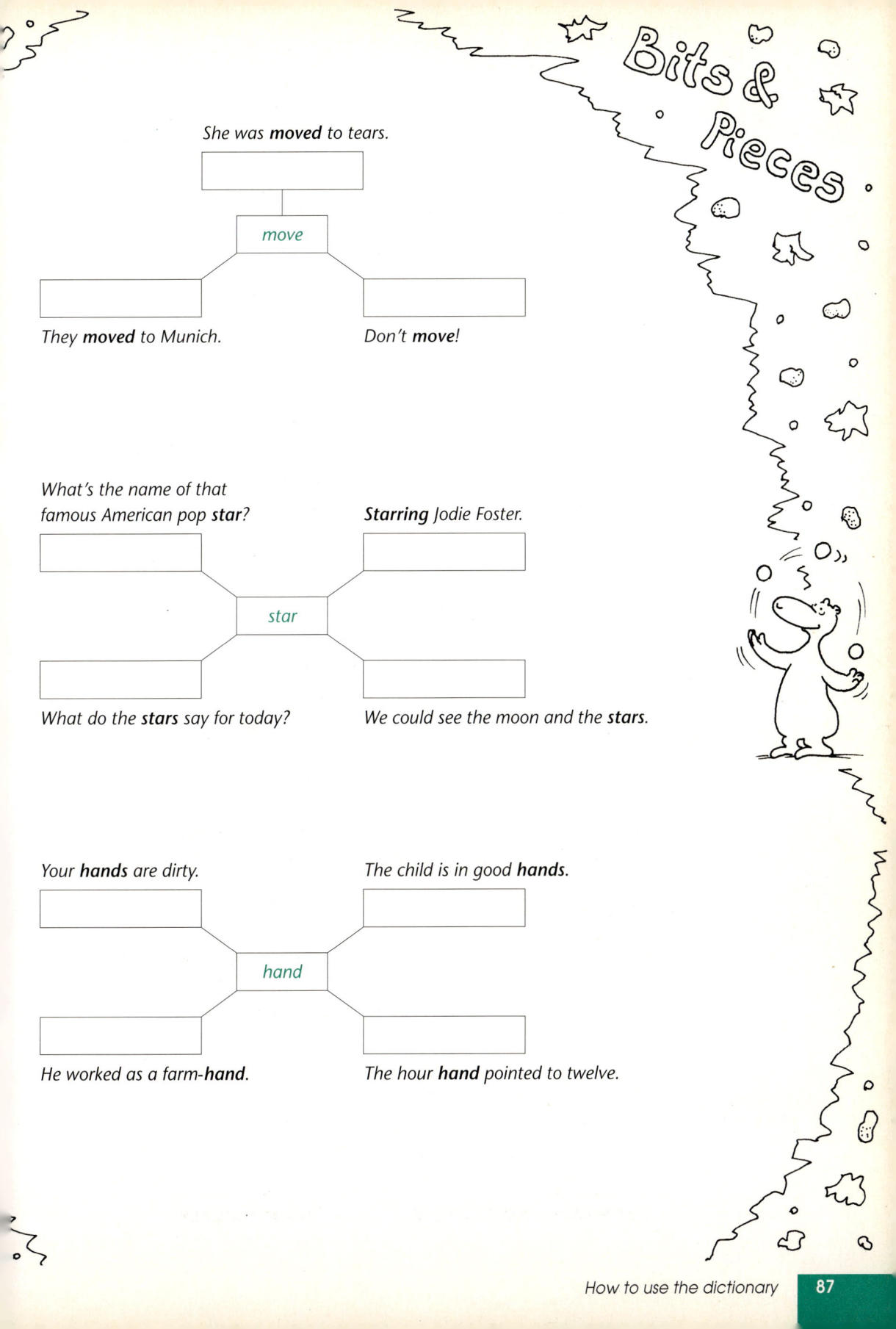

She was **moved** to tears.

move

They **moved** to Munich.

Don't **move**!

What's the name of that famous American pop **star**?

Starring Jodie Foster.

star

What do the **stars** say for today?

We could see the moon and the **stars**.

Your **hands** are dirty.

The child is in good **hands**.

hand

He worked as a farm-**hand**.

The hour **hand** pointed to twelve.

How to use the dictionary   87

F Some – any, much – many: Unbestimmte Pronomen
Indefinite pronouns

Some *oder* any? Much *oder* many? Each *oder* every? *Das ist häufig die Frage.*
In diesem Kapitel lernst du, die richtige Wahl zu treffen!

1. some – any

I bought some fantastic shirts in London.
I didn't buy any shoes.

Sicher ist dir die Faustregel geläufig:

some steht in bejahten Aussagesätzen, *any* in verneinten Aussagesätzen.

Da du jetzt schon zu den fortgeschrittenen EnglischlernerInnen gehörst, gibst du dich natürlich mit den ganz einfachen Erklärungsmustern nicht mehr so leicht zufrieden. Daher wollen wir in diesem Abschnitt einige Ergänzungen anfügen, um das Bild von *some* und *any* abzurunden.

Alles, was du jetzt liest, gilt übrigens für alle Zusammensetzungen mit *some* und *any*. Du kennst sie ja bereits:

some → body / one / thing / where   any → body / one / thing / where

Zunächst einige Anmerkungen zu *some*:

a) *I heard a noise. Is there somebody in the room?*
b) *Would you like some tea?*
   Wouldn't it be nice to invite some guests for dinner?

Regel

Some verwendest du
a) in **Fragesätzen**, wenn du als **Antwort „ja"** erwartest,
b) in **Fragesätzen**, die eine **Bitte**, eine **Einladung** oder ein **Angebot** darstellen.

88   Unbestimmte Pronomen

Weiter mit *any*:

Is there any soup left?
Aren't there any glasses in the cupboard?

> **Regel**
>
> Du verwendest *any* in **Fragesätzen**, wenn du **nicht sicher** bist, ob die Antwort „ja" oder „nein" lauten wird.

You can call me at any time.   jederzeit; egal, zu welcher Zeit

I want to go anywhere as long as it is warm.   wo immer; egal, wohin

Do your homework first. After that you can do anything you like!   alles; egal was

> **Regel**
>
> Du kannst *any* auch in bejahten Sätzen verwenden. Es bezeichnet dann eine **beliebige Sache** oder **Person**.
>
> | | |
> |---|---|
> | anybody | irgendjemand (egal, wer) |
> | anything | alles (egal, was) |
> | anywhere | überall (egal, wo/wohin) |

Nun zu unserem Übungsteil:

Kreuze das richtige Wort an und ergänze die Sätze. Manchmal gibt es auch zwei Möglichkeiten!

Exercise F 1

	some	somebody someone	something	somewhere
There is _____ in the car.				
Give me _____ apples, please.				
The camera must be _____.				
I want _____ to drink.				
There are _____ sausages left.				
_____ is behind you.				
Let's meet _____ else.				
I've just bought _____ cheese.				
_____ is wrong with my watch.				

Unbestimmte Pronomen

	any	anybody anyone	any-thing	any-where
I don't know _____ here.				
Is there _____ money left?				
Has _____ got a hanky¹?				
Have you seen him _____?				
Is _____ wrong?				
I haven't got _____ sugar.				
That doesn't make _____ sense.				
_____ else?				
I haven't got _____ friends.				

1 ugs. Taschentuch

Exercise F 2

In der nächsten Übung kommen *some* und *any* (somebody, anybody, …) vermischt vor. Setze die richtige Form ein.

1. The box is empty. There isn't _____ in it.
2. There are _____ pencils on the writing-desk.
3. I need _____ to help me with the washing-up.
4. You can phone me at _____ time.
5. Why don't we go _____ else?
6. Can you see my purse _____?
7. Would you like _____ sandwiches?

Wortliste

Anstelle von *not … any* kann man auch *no…* sagen:

not any   = *no*
not anything = *nothing*
not anybody = *nobody, no one*
not anywhere = *nowhere*

90 Unbestimmte Pronomen

Sieh dir den folgenden Beispielsatz an und wandle dann die vorgegebenen Sätze entsprechend um:

Exercise F 3

1. There's nothing in it. — There isn't anything in it.
2. We can see it nowhere. ....
3. There are no stamps on the letter. ....
4. Nobody was in the room. ....
5. He does nothing all day. ....

2. each – every

"Fred goes jogging every day."

Fred has got an aquarium in his room. Each fish has got a name.

every

bezeichnet jede(n), jedes allgemein bzw. jede(n), jedes ohne Ausnahme.

each

heißt es, wenn es sich um eine begrenzte Anzahl handelt und jede(r), jedes Einzelne aus dieser Gruppe gemeint ist.

Some more examples:

Every house has got a roof.

Every child likes ice-cream.

I think everybody knows "Jingle Bells".

Each pupil in the class …

There are fifteen houses in this street.

Each door is painted in a different colour.

Unbestimmte Pronomen

Exercise F 4

What's the name of the game?

Fill in *each* or *every*:

.... (1) child in the U. S. A. knows this game. To play it, you need two teams. .... (2) team has nine players. The game is played on a large field. One player throws a ball, another player tries to hit it with a long wooden stick. In order to make a "run" a player must touch .... (3) of the four "bases". Almost .... (4) American high school has a ? team.

F 3. much – many – a lot (of)

"And the weather forecast said there wouldn't be much rain today!"

There weren't many people in the stadium.

> **!** Verwende *much* (viel) bei nichtzählbaren Substantiven.
>
> Verwende *many* (viele) bei zählbaren Substantiven.

Fred has got a lot of CDs.

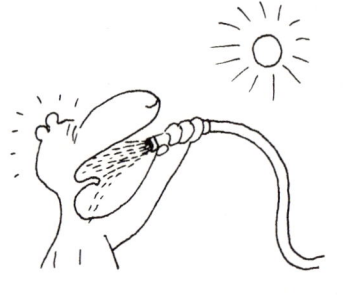

When it's hot Fred drinks a lot of water.

> **!** *A lot of* (oder etwas umgangssprachlicher: *lots of*) kannst du sowohl bei zählbaren als auch bei nichtzählbaren Substantiven verwenden.

Unbestimmte Pronomen

Sandra spends a lot of money on clothes.

There hasn't been a lot of sunshine lately.
There hasn't been much sunshine lately.

Did you get a lot of Valentine cards?
Did you get many Valentine cards?

In der Regel stehen *much* und *many* **nur in Fragesätzen und verneinten Sätzen**.
a lot of (lots of) steht in **bejahten und verneinten Aussagesätzen sowie in Fragesätzen**.

Fill in *much, many* or *a lot of*:

Jane's mother: What was the concert like? Were there .... (1) people?

Jane: Well, I met David, Linda and Michael in front of the concert hall. We were rather early, so at first there weren't .... (2) people. But after a while it got really crowded. I saw quite .... (3) boys and girls from my school. When the band came onto the stage, ... (4) fans moved forward, so there wasn't .... (5) space left. But the show was fantastic. They played .... (6) really good songs.

Exercise F 5

4. *(a) little – (a) few*

We had dinner in a nice little Italian restaurant.	… in einem netten kleinen italienischen Restaurant
Could I have a little milk, please?	… etwas / ein bisschen / ein wenig …
They had little hope of winning the match.	… wenig …

little vor einem **zählbaren Substantiv** bedeutet: klein

a little vor **unzählbaren Substantiven** heißt: etwas, ein bisschen

little vor einem **unzählbaren Substantiv** bedeutet: wenig

Unbestimmte Pronomen 93

I've got a few *pounds left.* … ein paar …

Few people *know that he's a millionaire.* … wenige …

> **!**
>
> *a few* steht **nur vor zählbaren Substantiven**:   ein paar, einige
>
> *few* steht ebenfalls **nur vor zählbaren Substantiven**:   wenige

few und *little* klingen oft etwas förmlich und können durch andere Ausdrücke ersetzt werden:

statt *few*:   *not many, hardly any*
statt *little*:   *not much, hardly any*

Auch hierzu eine kleine Übung:

A weekend trip

Exercise F 6

Fill in *(a) few* or *(a) little*:

My brother likes old castles, so we visited one at the weekend. I only know very _____ (1) about castle architecture, but my brother explained everything to us! There were only _____ (2) people around, so we could go wherever we liked. From the tower (236 steps to the top!) we had a wonderful view and we saw that there was _____ (3) lake nearby. I was _____ (4) tired after climbing up that tower. I said to the others that I would like to go down to the lake. Mum had made _____ (5) sandwiches and she had also packed some apples and a bottle of orange juice into _____ (6) basket. So we had a picnic by the lake.

Test

Für den Abschlusstest haben wir *some, any, each, every, much, many, a lot of, (a) few* and *(a) little* noch einmal gut durchgemischt. – Es ist angerichtet:

(Je 1 Punkt für jeden richtigen Ausdruck)

1. Hast du heute Nachmittag viel zu tun?

   Have you got _____ work to do this afternoon?

94   Unbestimmte Pronomen

2. Es tut mir Leid, ich habe keine Cola. Aber es ist etwas Milch im Kühlschrank. Wie wär's damit?

   I'm sorry, I haven't got .... coke. But there is .... milk in the fridge. How about that?

3. Gloria und Juliet gehen jeden Samstag zusammen zum Joggen.

   Gloria and Juliet go jogging together .... Saturday.

4. Möchtest du noch etwas Tee?

   Would you like .... more tea?

5. Verzeihung, wie komme ich bitte zum British Museum?
   – Sie können jeden beliebigen Bus von dieser Haltestelle aus nehmen.

   Excuse me, how can I get to the British Museum, please?

   – You can take .... bus from this stop.

6. Ms Redgrave hat fünf Katzen. Jede ihrer Katzen hat ein eigenes Körbchen.

   Ms Redgrave has five cats. .... of her cats has a basket of its own.

7. Wir hatten nicht viel Zeit, deshalb schrieben wir nur ein paar Postkarten.

   We didn't have .... time, so we only wrote .... postcards.

8. Ich war ein bisschen überrascht, als ich hörte, dass Rick die Fußballmannschaft verlassen hatte.

   I was .... surprised when I heard that Rick had left the football team.

Testauswertung

My personal scoreboard:

10–8 "right" scores:
Very good – you can be proud of yourself!

7–6 "right" scores:
Not too bad! Revise the indefinite pronouns that you got wrong.

5–0 "right" scores:
Have another look at the examples and exercises in this chapter. Then you will do better next time!

Unbestimmte Pronomen 95

Reading

Reading is good for your English! In fact, English is everywhere around you – just keep your eyes open. Here are some suggestions for your "reading list".

tins or packages

instructions

stage readers

English magazines

1 besser werden

Try to read English texts regularly. Even if you just read them for the fun of it and even if you don't look up every single word, your English will improve[1]. We would like to show you that you do not always have a look up a word in the dictionary in order to understand its meaning. And that makes reading a lot easier than you may have thought.

"Old Master" turned out to be a forgery

At a press conference held earlier this week the manager of a famous London art gallery announced that one of the old paintings that were to be sold to a rich American art collector was a forgery. A very good forgery, even experts had to admit!

Nobody would ever have found out if the collector from Boston had not seen the original at a friend's house some weeks before. Then exactly the same painting was offered to him in London.

Chemical tests proved that the art gallery only had a copy, and not the "Old Master". Specialists at Scotland Yard are now investigating the matter. Several people working at the gallery have been questioned so far.

Quite a number of private collectors as well as museums pay extra sums for expensive chemical tests to find out whether they, too, have a "Fake Master" on their wall!

Can cou guess what the words mean?

collector .... investigate ....

forgery .... chemical ....

How can you find out the meaning of a word?

The following check-list might help you:

1. Do I know a word from the same word family?
Fill in the missing words:

collector	collect	fame	....
painting	paint	follower	....
knowledge	....	changeable	....
meaningful	....	talkative	....

2. Is there a similar word in German?

chemical	chemisch	shoulder blade	....
information	Information	politician	....
decoration	....	repair	....
organize	....	mass media	....

3. Can I guess the meaning from the context?

"Old Master" turned out to be a forgery.

… the manager of a famous London art gallery announced that one of the old paintings that were to be sold to a rich American art collector was a forgery.

Well, you may not know what forgery means when reading the headline.

But from the context of the article it becomes quite clear that forgery means "Fälschung"!

You see – you don't have to look up every word you don't know. A bit of intelligent guessing can make life a lot easier!

Bits & Pieces

Reading 97

G Das Passiv
The passive

At a building site

In the street where Fred lives there's a building site[1].

In diesem Kapitel hast du Gelegenheit, die Bildung des Passivs in verschiedenen Zeiten zu üben.

1 Baustelle

Exercise G 1

Which of the following statements are true, which are false?

	true	false
1. When Fred came to the site this morning three walls had already been finished.	☐	☐
2. The cement was brought by a big cement mixer truck.	☐	☐
3. Most of the windows have already been put in.	☐	☐
4. Tomorrow the house will be finished.	☐	☐
5. Heavy parts are lifted by a crane.	☐	☐

Exercise G 2

Um welche Zeiten handelt es sich bei den Sätzen aus *Exercise 1*? Wenn dir die Namen der Zeiten nicht mehr geläufig sind, kannst du sie in Kapitel A nachlesen.

1. … three walls **had already been built**.   *Past Perfect*

2. The cement **was brought** …

3. … the windows **have already been put** in.

4. … the house **will be finished**.

5. Heavy parts **are lifted** …

Nun sehen wir uns die Bildung des Passivs etwas genauer an.

1. Die Zeitformen des Passivs
The tense forms of the passive

Hier siehst du eine Übersicht. Das Passiv wird immer mit einer Form des Verbs *(to) be* und dem *Past Participle* gebildet.

The wall	is	built ...	
The walls	are	built ...	*Present Tense*
The wall	was	built ...	
The walls	were	built ...	*Past Tense*
The wall	has been	built ...	
The walls	have been	built ...	*Present Perfect*
The wall(s)	had been	built ...	*Past Perfect*
The wall(s)	will be	built ...	*Future*
Subjekt	**Form des Verbs (to) be**	*Past Participle*	

In den folgenden Übungen kannst du das Passiv in verschiedenen Zeiten üben. Fangen wir mit der Gegenwart an.

Let's have a look at a garage. What is done here?

Übrigens:
Wenn du Vokabeln rund ums Auto wiederholen möchtest, wirf doch mal einen Blick auf die **Bits & Pieces**-Seiten 18/19.
Hier eine kleine Auswahl:

Exercise G 3

engine	*Motor*	plugs	*Zündkerzen*
tyres	*Reifen*	windscreen	
brakes	*Bremsen*	wipers	*Scheibenwischer*

1. engines/repair   Engines are repaired.

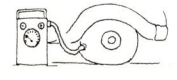

2. tyres/pump up   _____

Passiv

3. brakes/check ....

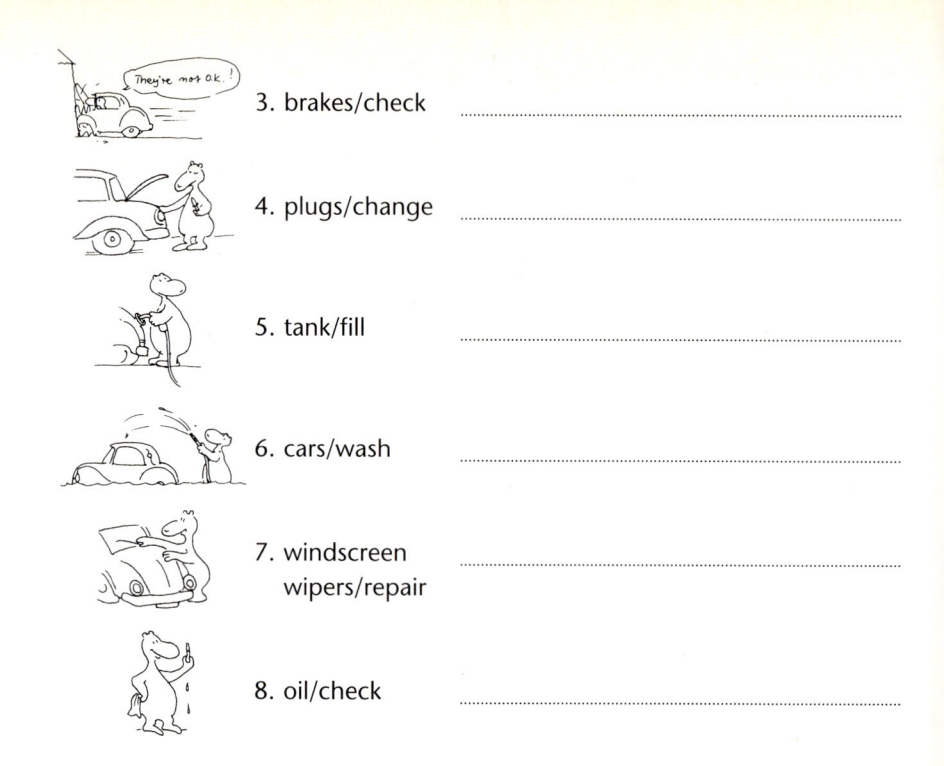

4. plugs/change ....

5. tank/fill ....

6. cars/wash ....

7. windscreen wipers/repair ....

8. oil/check ....

Da diese Arbeiten in einer Werkstatt Tag für Tag erledigt werden, steht hier immer **Simple Present**.
Wenn wir uns jedoch eine ganz bestimmte Szene ansehen, die sich gerade im Moment abspielt, muss auch im Passiv die **Progressive Form** stehen.

Was passiert gerade in der folgenden Szene?

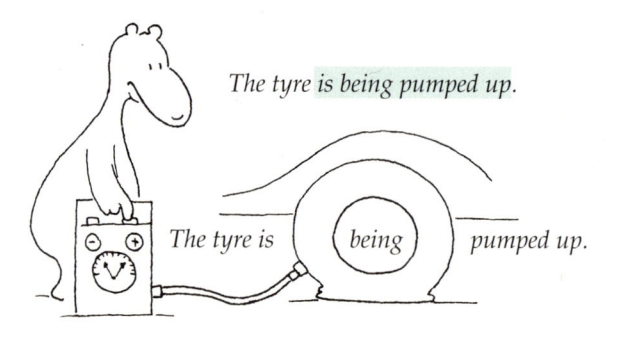

The tyre is being pumped up.

The tyre is | being | pumped up.

! Schiebe *being* zwischen *am/is/are* / *was/were* und *Past Participle* –
und schon hast du die Verlaufsform des Passivs!
Die Verlaufsform des Passivs kommt nur im *Present Tense* und im *Past Tense* vor.

What is being done in the following picture?

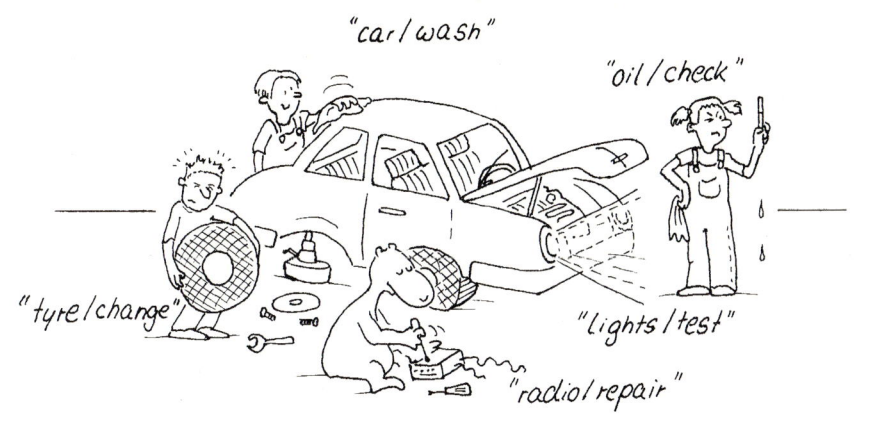

"car / wash"
"oil / check"
"tyre / change"
"lights / test"
"radio / repair"

Exercise G 4

1. The tyres ....
2. The car ....
3. The radio ....
4. The oil ....
5. The lights ....

And here is another good exercise:
Whenever you come across a picture (e. g. in a magazine), why don't you name the things that are being done?!

In der nächsten Übung geht es um die Vergangenheit.

> Florida was hit hardest by hurricane "Bonny". Hundreds of houses **were damaged**. It seems like a miracle that nobody **was killed**.

Exercise G 5

Fill in the correct passive forms of the verbs in brackets.

1. 52 persons *(injure)* ....

2. A bus *(sweep)*[1] .... off the road.   *1 (to) sweep-swept-swept: fegen*

3. Cars *(overturn)* ....

4. Trees *(uproot)*[2] ....   *2 entwurzeln*

5. A bridge *(destroy)* ....

6. The fire department *(call)* ....
   twenty-seven times last night.

Passiv

A burglary

Exercise G 6

Mr and Mrs Townsend have just come home from the theatre. When they enter their living room they are shocked. There has been a burglary. They call the police immediately. One of the policemen makes some notes.

Complete the sentences.

1. The living room window *(break)* has been broken.
2. The wardrobe *(open)* _____.
3. All the clothes *(throw)* _____ on the floor.
4. Papers *(tear)* _____ to pieces.
5. The TV set *(smash up)* _____.
6. The silver candle sticks *(take away)* _____.
7. The stamp collection *(steal)* _____.
8. A bottle of whisky *(drink)* _____.
9. The radio *(damage)* _____.

Exercise G 7

A few days after the burglary Mr and Mrs Townsend are talking to their neighbour: "We came home from the theatre at about eleven o'clock. When we entered the living room we both couldn't believe what we saw –

The window had been broken.
The wardrobe ..."

Go on. Look at the sentences above and use the *past perfect* this time.

102 Passiv

Eine Übung zum Futur findest du an späterer Stelle in diesem Kapitel. Jetzt geht es zunächst weiter mit der Frage: Wie unterscheiden sich die Formen von Aktiv und Passiv?

2. Aktiv und Passiv
Active and passive

Das Verb *(to) be* spielt sowohl bei der Bildung von Aktiv- als auch von Passiv-Formen eine wichtige Rolle. Auf den ersten Blick scheint es schwierig, all die verschiedenen Möglichkeiten auseinander zu halten. Aber du wirst sehen – Übung schafft den Durchblick!

Du hast das Verb *(to) be* bisher verwendet

als **Vollverb**:

*This **is** my pen.*	ist
*Here **are** your books.*	sind
*They **were** in London.*	waren

als Teil der **Progressive Form**:

*Fred **is** making a pancake.*	macht gerade
*Ann **was** playing tennis.*	spielte gerade

Nun kommt das **Passiv** hinzu:

*Fred **is** often asked …*	wird oft gefragt
*The windows **were** shut.*	wurden geschlossen
*The car **will be** sold.*	wird verkauft werden

In dieser Übung sollst du nun feststellen,

- ob es sich um Aktiv oder Passiv handelt und
- in welcher Zeit die Sätze stehen.

Exercise G 8

	Active/Passive	Tense
Tom is writing a letter.	Active	Present
This machine was built in the USA.		
This parcel has been opened before.		
My friend has often been in London.		
These recorders are made in Japan.		
We are making a doll.		
The car was stolen last night.		
They were very happy.		
The books were read by many people.		
Your father will be very angry.		
A new hotel will be built in our street.		

Oft kann man einen Aktiv-Satz in eine Passiv-Konstruktion umformen – und umgekehrt. Hier ein Beispiel:

Aktiv:
A famous pop star will sing the national anthem.

Passiv:
The national anthem will be sung by a famous pop star.
(von …)

Regel

Aus dem **Akkusativobjekt des Aktivsatzes** (wen oder was?) **wird** das **Subjekt des Passivsatzes** (wer oder was?).

Aus dem Subjekt des Aktivsatzes *(A famous pop star)* wird im Passivsatz: **by** *a famous pop star.*

Passiv

Change the following sentences from the active into the passive voice. Use the same tense as in the given sentence.

Exercise G 9

1. A lot of newspaper editors printed President Clinton's speech.

   President Clinton's speech was printed by a lot of newspaper editors.

2. Thousands of people visit Ailwee Cave every summer.

   ....

3. The magician cut Fred in two.

   ....

4. Four waiters had brought in the wedding cake.

   ....

5. More than 200,000 people have already bought the new Madonna CD.

   ....

   ....

6. The French team won the World Cup in 1998.

   ....

7. The mayor will open the exhibition next Friday.

   ....

Passiv

3. Das Passiv in Verbindung mit *can, must* und *may*
The passive in connection with can, must and may

Sehen wir uns noch einmal auf der Baustelle in der Nähe von Freds Zuhause um:

*At the building site helmets **must be worn** by everybody.*

! In Verbindung mit *can, must* und *may* wird das Passiv so gebildet:

Lots of things **can be seen** …
 … können gesehen werden

Helmets **must be worn** …
 … müssen getragen werden

Photos **may be taken** …
 … dürfen gemacht werden

Rubbish **mustn't be thrown** …
 … darf nicht geworfen werden

Diese Beispielsätze stehen im *Present Tense*. In anderen Zeiten musst du die jeweiligen Ersatzformen von *can, must* und *may* verwenden. Du findest alles Wichtige zu diesen drei unvollständigen Hilfsverben im Abschnitt D dieses Buches.

Einige Formen, die du vielleicht häufiger benötigst, haben wir hier für dich zusammengestellt:

Helmets **must be worn** … / **have to be worn** …   *Present Tense*
 … müssen getragen werden …

Helmets **needn't be worn** … / **don't have to be worn** …
 … müssen nicht getragen werden …

  … **had to be worn** …   *Past Tense*
 … mussten getragen werden …

  … **didn't have to be worn** …
 … mussten nicht getragen werden …

106 Passiv

Fred can be found ...   ... kann gefunden werden ...   **Present Tense**

Fred can't be found ...   ... kann nicht gefunden werden ...

Fred could be found ...   ... konnte gefunden werden ...   **Past Tense**

Fred couldn't be found ... ... konnte nicht gefunden werden ...

Die Ersatzformen klingen hier eher umständlich und werden daher kaum verwendet.

Mit der folgenden Übung kannst du überprüfen, ob du auch diesen Bereich des Passivs bereits beherrschst.

1 to keep on the lead
2 microware (oven)
3 to bandage *(regular)*
4 paintings
5 flash
6 oysters
7 to pull out a tooth

Übersetze ins Englische:

Exercise G 10

1. Hunde müssen an der Leine[1] geführt werden.

   ....

2. Die Patienten dürfen von 16.00 bis 19.00 Uhr besucht werden.

   ....

3. Die Fenster konnten nicht geöffnet werden.

   ....

4. Rohe Eier dürfen nicht in der Mikrowelle[2] erhitzt werden.

   ....

5. Freds Bein musste verbunden[3] werden.

   ....

6. Die Gemälde[4] dürfen nicht mit Blitz[5] fotografiert werden.

   ....

7. Austern[6] können roh gegessen werden.

   ....

8. Gott sei Dank musste der Zahn nicht gezogen[7] werden!

   ....

Passiv

4. Das persönliche Passiv
The personal passive

Zum Schluss hast du noch Gelegenheit, eine Form des Passivs zu üben, die sich vom Deutschen unterscheidet: das persönliche Passiv.

Aus dem folgenden Satz lässt sich – du weißt ja bereits wie – ganz leicht ein Passiv konstruieren:

A nice lady offered me a piece of cake.

Subjekt — Akkusativobjekt

A piece of cake was offered to me (by a nice lady).

Man nehme das Akkusativobjekt des Aktiv-Satzes und mache es zum Subjekt des Passiv-Satzes.

Es gibt aber noch eine weitere Möglichkeit:

A nice lady offered me a piece of cake.

Subjekt — Dativobjekt

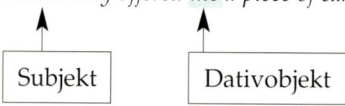

I was offered a piece of cake (by a nice lady).

> Auch das **Dativobjekt** (wem oder was?) eines **Aktiv-Satzes** kann im **Passiv-Satz zum Subjekt** werden.

Im Deutschen kann man nicht sagen: Ich wurde ein Stück Kuchen angeboten. Vielmehr muss es heißen: Mir wurde ein Stück Kuchen angeboten.

Dazu gleich eine Übung:

Exercise G 11

1. Granny told <u>Tom</u> an interesting story.

   Tom ....

2. Mr Brown had sold <u>Mr Smith</u> the old Ford.

   Mr Smith ....

3. A friendly gentleman showed <u>me</u> the way.

   I ....

4. One of her friends has sent <u>Barbara</u> a postcard from Australia.

   Barbara ....

5. The stewardess gave <u>me</u> a glass of orange juice.

   I ....

Wie angekündigt, hier nun eine Übung zum Futur, in der auch gelegentlich ein persönliches Passiv vorkommt.

A cycling tour through Ireland

Exercise G 12

The Greenfields from Boston are planning a two weeks' cycling tour through Ireland. Their bikes will be transported on the plane, together with the other baggage[1]. In Ireland someone will
– pick them up at Dublin airport,
– take them and the baggage to a guesthouse,
– give them special cycling maps,
– transport their baggage from one guesthouse to the next,
– book their rooms in advance,
– show them where to put their bikes,
– tell them where to find inns or coffee shops on the way.

1 baggage – (Amer. Engl.) Gepäck

Cathy Greenfield is telling her friend Sue about the trip:

We will be picked up at Dublin airport.

We ....

We ....

Our baggage ....

Our rooms ....

We ....

We ....

Bevor du den gewohnten Abschlusstest absolvierst, solltest du noch einmal die verschiedenen Formen des Passivs wiederholen. Damit das Ganze nicht zu unübersichtlich wird, enthält die folgende Tabelle nur die *Simple Forms*; die *Progressive Forms* wurden hier nicht berücksichtigt.

Ergänze die fehlenden Formen:

Exercise G 13

Past Perfect	Simple Past	Present Perfect	Simple Present	Future I
it had been stolen				
	he was found			
		we have been asked		
			she is seen	
				it will be sold
			it is made	
		it has been used		
	it was written			
they had been repaired				

Und wie am Ende jedes Kapitels kannst du auch jetzt wieder deine Kenntnisse überprüfen.

Test

Change the following sentences into the passive voice.
(Je 2 Punkte für jeden richtigen Satz, davon 1 Punkt für die richtige Verbform und 1 Punkt für den Rest)

1. Dad will pick you up at the airport.

   ....

2. Mr Brown has often repaired the car himself.

   ....

3. People all over the world drink tea.

   ....

Passiv

4. Skyline Enterprises offered Mrs Barnes a leading position.

   Mrs Barnes

5. David Bowie had written the soundtrack.

6. The firemen had to rescue four people and a cat from the burning house.

Translate the following advert for the latest Hollywood film:
(Die maximale Punktzahl steht jeweils in Klammern.)

1 creatures
2 fast-food restaurant

Der spannendste Film, der jemals gemacht wurde!	(2)
Amerika wird von gefährlichen Wesen[1] angegriffen.	(2)
Sie wurden geschickt, um alle Schnellimbiss-Restaurants[2] mitzunehmen.	(2)
Wenn sie nicht aufgehalten werden können, wird New York zerstört werden!	(3)
Ein Held muss gefunden werden, der gegen diese Wesen kämpfen wird.	(2)
Er ist gefunden worden: Fred, der Terminator!	(1)

Testauswertung

My personal scoreboard:

24–19 "right" scores:
Brilliant! You did a really good job!
You know all the tenses well, and more than that – you use the passive as if it was the easiest thing in the world.

18–12 "right" scores:
That's a good score for such a difficult matter! If you had problems with the tenses, read chapter A. If you feel uneasy about the passive, do some of the exercises in this chapter again.

11–0 "right" scores:
Make sure you know how to form the tenses (Chapter A) before reading this chapter carefully again. Do all the exercises – then try the test again.

Unregelmäßige Verben

Bestimmt kennst du Bilderbücher, bei denen man einzelne Teile umklappen kann. Dadurch entstehen lustige Tiere.

Diese Idee machen wir uns für unser erstes Lernspiel zunutze und nennen es:

1. Flippy Verbs

Besorge dir im Schreibwarengeschäft etwas festeres (farbiges) Papier. Du kannst es in großen Bögen kaufen, die du dann so lange halbierst, bis Blätter in DIN A5 daraus geworden sind. Beschrifte die einzelnen Blätter folgendermaßen:

Schreibe dabei jedes unregelmäßige Verb auf ein einzelnes Blatt. Lege auch einige leere Blätter dazu (für Verben, die du im Lauf des Schuljahres noch lernst) und lass im Schreibwarengeschäft oder Kopierladen eine Spirale einziehen. Anschließend kannst du jedes Blatt an den gestrichelten Linien (siehe Muster) durchschneiden.

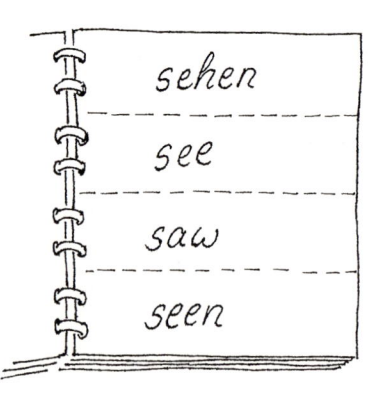

Jetzt kann's losgehen!

Blättere einen der Abschnitte beliebig oft um. Vielleicht steht darauf:

Ergänze nun alle Formen dieses Verbs, indem du sie laut vor dich hin sagst und anschließend die anderen Stapel entsprechend umblätterst.

112 Unregelmäßige Verben

2. Verben-Kartei

Wenn dir unser erster Vorschlag zu aufwendig ist, kannst du die unregelmäßigen Verben natürlich auch auf Karteikarten oder farbige Zettel schreiben.

Etwa so: Vorderseite Rückseite

gehen

go – went – gone

Deine Verben-Kartei lässt sich jederzeit beliebig erweitern.

Willst du nicht nur die unregelmäßigen Verbformen, sondern auch die Zeiten wiederholen, wie wär's mit folgender Übung:

3. Würfelspiel

Jede Zahl auf dem Würfel steht für eine bestimmte Zeit:

- ⚀ Will-Future
- ⚁ Present Tense
- ⚂ Past Tense
- ⚃ Present Perfect
- ⚄ Past Perfect
- ⚅ Free Choice (Freie Auswahl)

Ziehe eine Karte aus deiner Verben-Kartei und würfle eine Zahl. Setze nun das Verb in die entsprechende Zeit. Dabei kannst du die Person (I, you, he, she, it, we, you, they) selbst bestimmen. Würfelst du eine 6, darfst du dir eine Zeit aussuchen.

Ein Beispiel:

werfen

I have thrown

Zwei Spieler(innen) können sich abwechseln oder gegeneinander antreten. Wer weniger Fehler macht, gewinnt.
Ihr könnt auch festlegen, dass in der nächsten Runde die *Progressive Form* in den entsprechenden Zeiten verwendet werden muss oder die Zeitformen des Passivs gebildet werden müssen.

Unregelmäßige Verben

H Indirekte Rede: Fragesätze und Befehlssätze
Reported speech: Questions and commands

Bevor wir uns mit indirekten Fragen und Befehlssätzen beschäftigen, sollten wir eine kurze Wiederholung einschieben. Wie war das doch gleich mit der Zeitenfolge bei Aussagesätzen in der indirekten Rede?

In diesem Kapitel lernst du, Fragen und Befehle in der indirekten Rede wiederzugeben.

Zeichne Pfeile ein, um die Zeitverschiebung in der indirekten Rede zu verdeutlichen, wenn das einleitende Verb in der Vergangenheit steht.

Exercise H 1

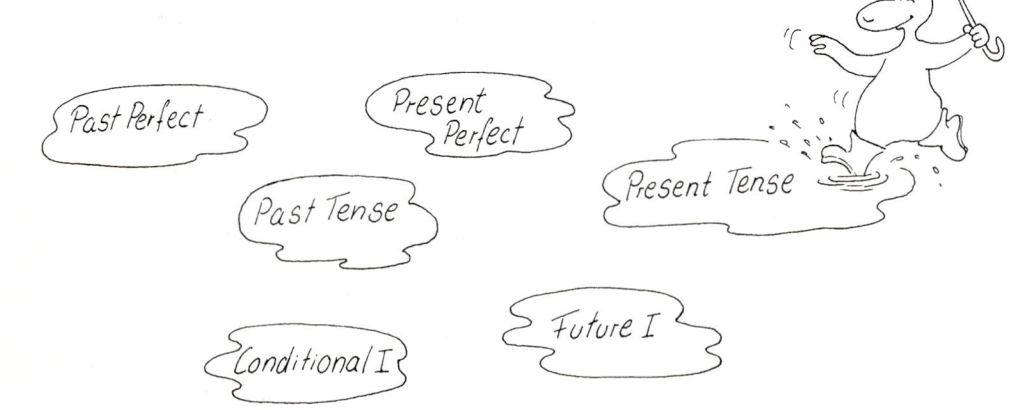

Past Perfect
Present Perfect
Past Tense
Present Tense
Conditional I
Future I

he said

Wie müssen also die folgenden Aussagen als indirekte Rede lauten?

1. Kevin: "I'll meet you at the station."

   Kevin said to his cousin (that) ....

   ....

2. Mrs Winter: "There is a new Mexican restaurant in Regent Street. I've always wanted to try tortillas."

   ....

   ....

3. Susan: "At the weekend we went on a cycling tour. We didn't get very far – it started to rain ten minutes after we had left."

....

....

4. Tom: "The driver of the red Ford hadn't indicated[1]. He turned right rather abruptly."

1 geblinkt

....

....

Hattest du Schwierigkeiten, die Sätze umzuformen? Dann solltest du dir zuerst Kapitel E vornehmen.
Oder war für dich alles sonnenklar? – Dann kann's gleich weitergehen!

1. Fragen in der indirekten Rede
Questions in indirect speech

Vor dem Supermarkt, in dem auch Fred oft einkauft, wird eine Umfrage durchgeführt.

1. *How old are you?*
2. *Why did you come here?*
3. *How often do you come here?*
4. *How long have you been here?*
5. *Do you buy all your things here?*
6. *Do you have a car?*
7. *Do you park your car in the supermarket car park?*

The next day Fred tells his friend Ron:

"*At the supermarket they carried out a survey[2]. A young man interviewed Mrs Moore.*

1. *First he wanted to know how old she was.*
2. *Then he asked her why she had gone there.*
3. *Then he asked her how often she went there.*
4. *And he asked how long she had been there.*
5. *He wanted to know if she bought all her things there.*
6. *He also wanted to know if she had a car and*
7. *whether she parked her car in the supermarket car park.*"

2 eine Umfrage durchführen

Indirekte Rede: Frage- und Befehlssätze **115**

Exercise H 2

Unterstreiche in den Sätzen 1. bis 7. jeweils alle Verbformen.

Das einleitende Verb steht in der unteren Gruppe immer im *Past Tense*. Wie verändern sich die Zeiten in der indirekten Rede?

Present Tense ⟶ ....

Past Tense ⟶ ....

Present Perfect ⟶ ....

Gilt die Zeitenfolge, wie du sie für Aussagesätze gelernt hast, auch für indirekte Fragesätze?

☐ Ja.   ☐ Nein.

> **!** Die Zeitform des Verbs verändert sich in der indirekten Rede nur, wenn das **einleitende Verb in der Vergangenheit** steht. Steht es in der Gegenwart, dann bleibt die Zeit in der indirekten Rede dieselbe wie in der wörtlichen Rede.

Ein Beispiel:

Is everything alright, Marvin?

Mum always asks if everything is alright, when she knows that nothing is alright!

Betrachten wir nun die Satzstellung in der wörtlichen beziehungsweise in der indirekten Rede etwas genauer. Bei den Fragen haben wir es mit zwei verschiedenen Arten zu tun:

– **mit Entscheidungsfragen** *(yes/no questions)*:

Hilfsverb	Subjekt	Verb	Objekt
Do / Does / Have	you / he / you	like / know / seen	

Indirekte Rede: Frage- und Befehlssätze

– oder mit Fragen, die durch ein Fragewort eingeleitet werden:

Fragewort	Hilfsverb	Subjekt	Verb	(Objekt)
Why / How old / How long	did / are / have	she / you / you	come / been	

In der indirekten Rede sehen die Fragen dann so aus:

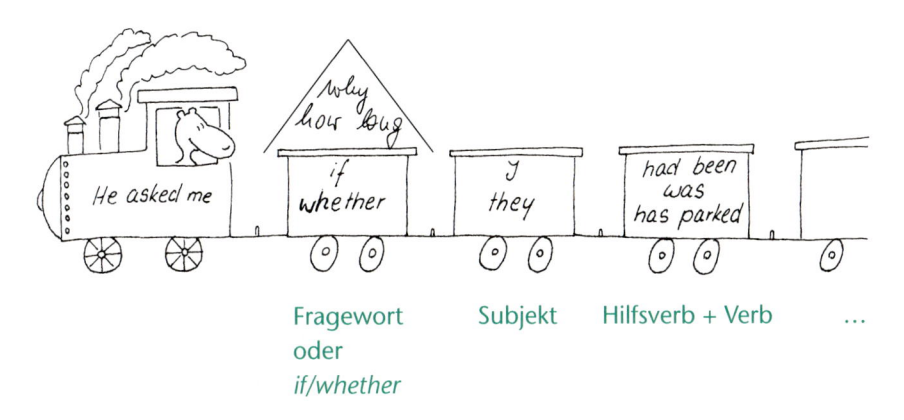

He asked me | why / how long / if / whether | I / they | had been / was / has parked | ...

Fragewort oder *if/whether* | Subjekt | Hilfsverb + Verb | ...

Die Fragewörter der wörtlichen Rede tauchen auch in der indirekten Rede wieder auf:

How old …?	*… wanted to know*	*how old …*
Why …?		*why …*
How often …?	*… asked me*	*how often …*
How long …?		*how long …*

Entscheidungsfragen
beginnen in der wörtlichen Rede mit einem Hilfsverb: | In der indirekten Rede werden sie mit *if* bzw. *whether* eingeleitet:

Did you buy …?	*… asked me*	*if/whether I had bought …*
Do you like …?		*I liked …*
Have you seen …?	*… wanted to know*	*if/whether I had seen …*
Can you swim?		*I could swim.*

Beachte, dass in indirekten Fragen das Subjekt vor dem Hilfsverb bzw. Verb steht (wie in Aussagesätzen)!
Die Umschreibung mit *do/does/did* entfällt im indirekten Fragesatz!

Indirekte Rede: Frage- und Befehlssätze 117

Hier noch einmal die wichtigsten Regeln in Kurzform:

Regel

Indirekte Fragesätze (einleitendes Verb in der Vergangenheit):
- Zeitenfolge beachten
- Umschreibung mit *do* entfällt
- Fragewörter bleiben
- bei Entscheidungsfragen *if* (oder *whether*) verwenden
- **Subjekt** steht **vor** dem (Hilfsverb +) Verb

Now it's your turn.
The pupils in Linda's class are working on a project called "Teenagers and Television". This is an extract from the questionnaire[1] they have put together:

Exercise H 3

1 *Fragebogen*
2 *Kurzform von* **goggle box** = *die „Glotze"*

1. How many hours per day do you spend in front of the "box"[2]?
2. What did you watch yesterday?
   Which programmes?
   How long?
3. Are there any programmes you watch regularly?
4. Do you never/sometimes/often switch channels in the middle of a programme?
5. How many TV sets are there in your flat/house?
6. Have you got a TV set of your own?

3 **telly** = **television**

7. Have you ever switched off the telly[3] because you didn't like the film/programme?   ☐ Never.   ☐ Once or twice.   ☐ Often.
8. What do you do during commercial breaks?

Joe writes a report for the school magazine. (Complete the sentences!)

1. The first thing we wanted to know was how many hours per day the pupils .... in front of the "box".

2. We asked them ....

3. and ....

4. We also wanted to find out ....

   ....

5. Of course we asked ....

   ....

6. and ....

118 Indirekte Rede: Frage- und Befehlssätze

7. Apart from that we wanted to know ....

....

8. and ....

Und wie sehen deine Fernsehgewohnheiten aus? – Why don't **you** answer the questions of the questionnaire?! Say what kinds of programmes you often/sometimes/never watch etc.!

Here is some vocabulary that might be useful:

Wortliste

sports (programme)	Sport(sendung)
news (programme)	Nachrichten(sendung)
documentary	Reportage, Bericht
situation comedy	lustige Familiensendung
series, serial	Serie
detective film	Krimi
music programme	Musiksendung
game show	Spielshow
movie	Spielfilm

Und jetzt gleich noch eine Übung zu den indirekten Fragesätzen. Diesmal sollst du vom Deutschen ins Englische übersetzen.

A star is born

Daisy Doolittle möchte eine berühmte Schauspielerin werden. Sie erzählt ihrer Freundin von ihrem Gespräch mit einem Produzenten:

Exercise H 4

Übersetze:

1. Er wollte wissen, ob ich singen könne.

....

....

2. Er fragte mich, in welchen Stücken ich schon gespielt hätte.

....

3. Dann fragte er mich, ob ich an einer Rolle interessiert wäre und ob ich am Dienstag ins Studio kommen könnte.

....

....

Übrigens: Daisy bekam die Rolle!

Indirekte Rede: Frage- und Befehlssätze

2. Befehlssätze in der indirekten Rede
The imperative in indirect speech

Beim Drehen des Werbespots musste Daisy Doolittle eine ganze Reihe von Anweisungen befolgen:

> Don't speak too fast!

> Sing a little tune!

> Move to the right and hold up the tin of catfood.

> Don't walk like a model!

> Look at the cat after saying your sentence.

Am Abend erzählt sie ihrer Freundin von ihrem anstrengenden Drehtag:

> The director asked me to sing a little tune.

> He wanted me to move to the right and hold up the tin of catfood.

> The assistant wanted me to look at the cat.

> She told me not to walk like a model.

> He ordered me not to speak too fast.

Die wörtlichen Befehlssätze beginnen jeweils mit einem Imperativ:

Move to the right …
Don't speak …

> **Regel**
>
> Der indirekte Befehlssatz wird mit einem Verb des Befehlens eingeleitet. Danach steht die Person, der der Befehl gegeben wurde, und der Infinitiv des Verbs:

…asked	me	to sing …	…bat mich … zu singen
…told	me	not to walk …	…sagte mir, ich solle nicht …
…wanted	me	to move …	…wollte, dass ich … gehe.
…ordered	me	not to speak …	…gab mir die Anweisung/befahl mir, nicht … zu sprechen.

! Übrigens spielt es hier keine Rolle, in welcher Zeit das einleitende Verb steht. – Der indirekte Befehlssatz sieht immer gleich aus:

My mum always tells me to eat slowly.
   Meine Mutter sagt mir immer, ich solle langsam essen.

My mum told me to eat slowly.
   Meine Mutter sagte mir, ich solle langsam essen.

Natürlich kann man einen indirekten Befehlssatz auch umständlicher mit *should* bilden:

My dad said that I should switch off the TV.

Eleganter klingt jedoch die Version:

My dad told me to switch off the TV.

Indirekte Rede: Frage- und Befehlssätze

Exercise H 5

Jetzt wird es aber höchste Zeit für eine Übung!

Ann kommt eine Dreiviertelstunde später als vereinbart zu ihrer Freundin Sally.

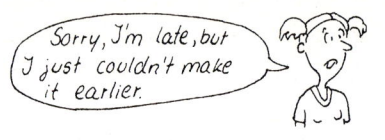

Sorry, I'm late, but I just couldn't make it earlier.

1. First, Tim asked me ....

2. Then Mum wanted me ....

3. Grandma ....

4. The worst thing was that Mum ordered me ....

5. Then Andy came in and ....

6. When I said goodbye, Dad ....

Exercise H 6

The next day Sally's mother asked why Ann had been so late the day before. Sally said:

"Well, first Tim asked her to help him with his maths homework. Then her mum

....
....
....
....
....
....

Indirekte Rede: Frage- und Befehlssätze

At the doctor's

Dies ist eine gemischte Übung, in der sowohl Aussagesätze als auch Fragen und Befehle vorkommen. Wenn du die bisherigen Übungen zur indirekten Rede gut durchgearbeitet hast, wird sie dir sicherlich keine Schwierigkeiten machen.

Lies zunächst den Dialog zwischen dem Arzt und einem Patienten durch.

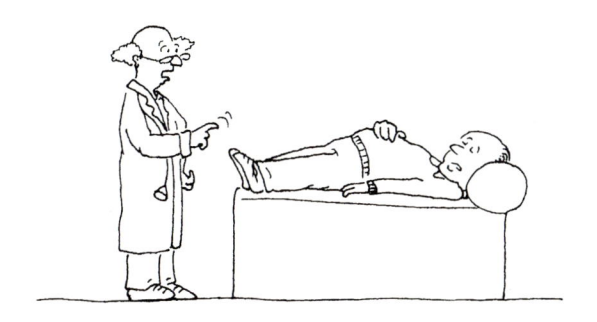

Exercise H 7

Why have you come here?

    I don't feel very well.

Stand up, please.
Bend your knees!
Now please lie down on this couch.
Do you often drink alcohol?

    Oh, yes. I have some bottles of beer every night.

Where do you have lunch!

    There is a canteen at my office.
    I have a hot meal there every day.

Does your wife cook a hot meal for you in the evening?

    Oh, yes, she is a splendid cook.

What did you do last weekend?

    I watched TV. There were some good films on.

When did you last go for a walk?

    I don't know. I have never liked doing that.

I think I know what's wrong with you: you eat too much!

Have only one hot meal a day, eat more fruit and try to go for a walk every day. You'll feel much better after that.

Indirekte Rede: Frage- und Befehlssätze

At home Mr Lazy told his wife:

"I'll never go to that doctor again! He didn't give me any medicine, he only asked and told me a lot of silly things!

1. First he asked me ....
2. I told him that I ....
3. After that he ordered ....
4. Then he wanted ....
5. He wanted to know ....
6. I said to him ....
7. He asked me ....
8. and I told him ....
....
9. He asked me ....
10. I answered that ....
11. Then he wanted to know ....
12. I told him ....
13. He then asked me ....
14. and I replied ....
15. Then he said ....
....
16. He told me ....
....
...."

Hast du das Gefühl, dass du alles bereits gut beherrschst? Dann mache jetzt zum Abschluss unseren Test.

Wenn dir der eine oder andere Aspekt der indirekten Fragen oder Befehlssätze noch Schwierigkeiten bereitet, schau dir noch einmal intensiv die jeweiligen Merksätze an und bearbeite einige der Übungen noch einmal. Dann wirst du topfit sein.

Indirekte Rede: Frage- und Befehlssätze

Test

(Je 2 Punkte für jeden richtigen Satz)

Übertrage die folgenden Sätze in die indirekte Rede:
Manchmal musst du ein anderes einleitendes Verb verwenden.

1. Shirley asked her friend: "Do you like my dress?"

   ....

2. The teacher told Mary: "Please repeat the sentence!"

   ....

3. The gangster shouted to the old lady: "Give me your handbag!"

   ....

   ....

4. The policeman asked the visitor: "Where did you see the man?"

   ....

5. Lisa's new classmates wanted to know: "Have you already been to the school cafeteria?"

   ....

   ....

6. Mrs Scott said to her little son: "Don't throw the peas on the floor!"

   ....

   ....

7. The boy said to his dog: "Bring me the ball!"

   ....

8. Paul asked Tim: "Are you tired?"

   ....

9. Fiona asked her aunt: "When will you go on holiday this year?"

   ....

10. Mr White said to his daughter: "Don't use my tie as a belt!"

    ....

Indirekte Rede: Frage- und Befehlssätze

Testauswertung

My personal scoreboard:

20–15 "right" scores:
You are the champion! You know how to form and use indirect questions and commands.

14–10 "right" scores:
That's a good result! Try to find out what sort of mistakes you made and decide in which field you need just a little more practice.

9–0 "right" scores:
O. K., that was just the warming-up round! Read this chapter carefully and do all the exercises. Then you will do much better next time!

Rechtschreibung

Die englische Rechtschreibung ist nicht immer einfach. Hier findest du einige Tipps, wie du dir die richtige Schreibweise mancher Wörter besser einprägen kannst.

1. Lernposter

Es gibt einige Rechtschreibregeln bzw. Besonderheiten, die sich gut und übersichtlich auf einem selbst gefertigten Lernposter darstellen lassen.

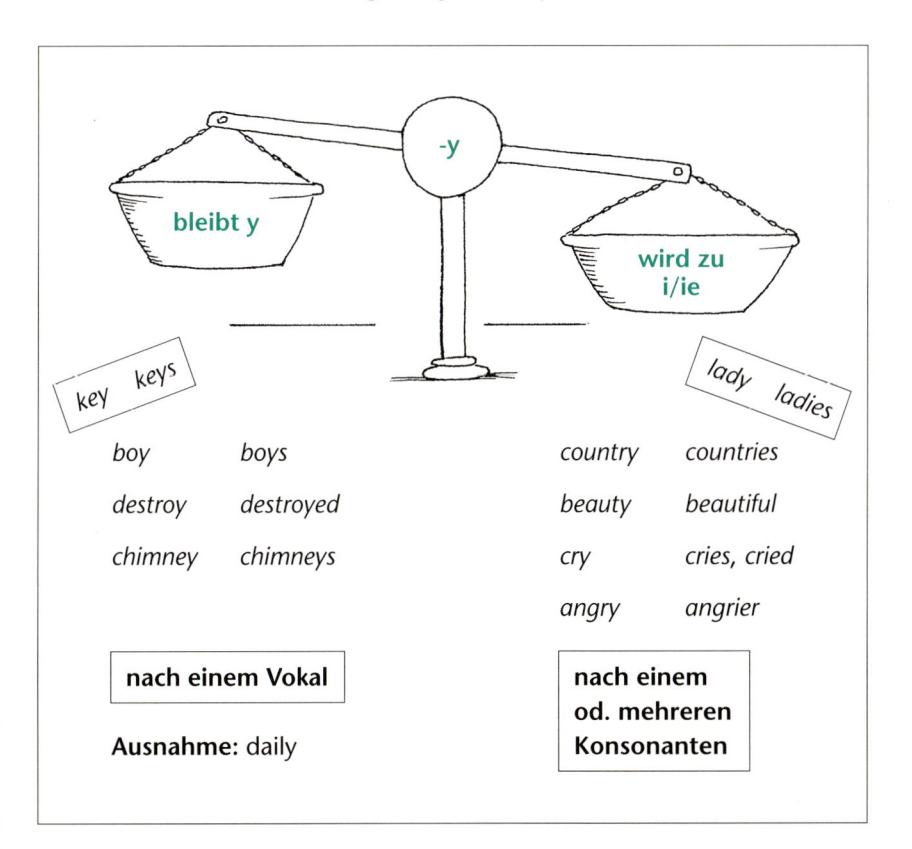

-y

bleibt y — **wird zu i/ie**

key   keys

boy   boys
destroy destroyed
chimney chimneys

lady   ladies

country   countries
beauty   beautiful
cry   cries, cried
angry   angrier

nach einem Vokal

Ausnahme: daily

nach einem od. mehreren Konsonanten

Wann immer dir ein Wort einfällt, das auf -y endet, kannst du dein Lernposter erweitern und z. B. kleine farbige Zettel darauf kleben (etwa gelbe für diejenigen Wörter, in denen das -y auch y bleibt, und grüne für Wörter, in denen das -y zu i/ie wird.

Probier's doch gleich mal aus! Vielleicht fallen dir zu jeder der beiden Gruppen je drei Wörter ein?!

2. Eselsbrücken

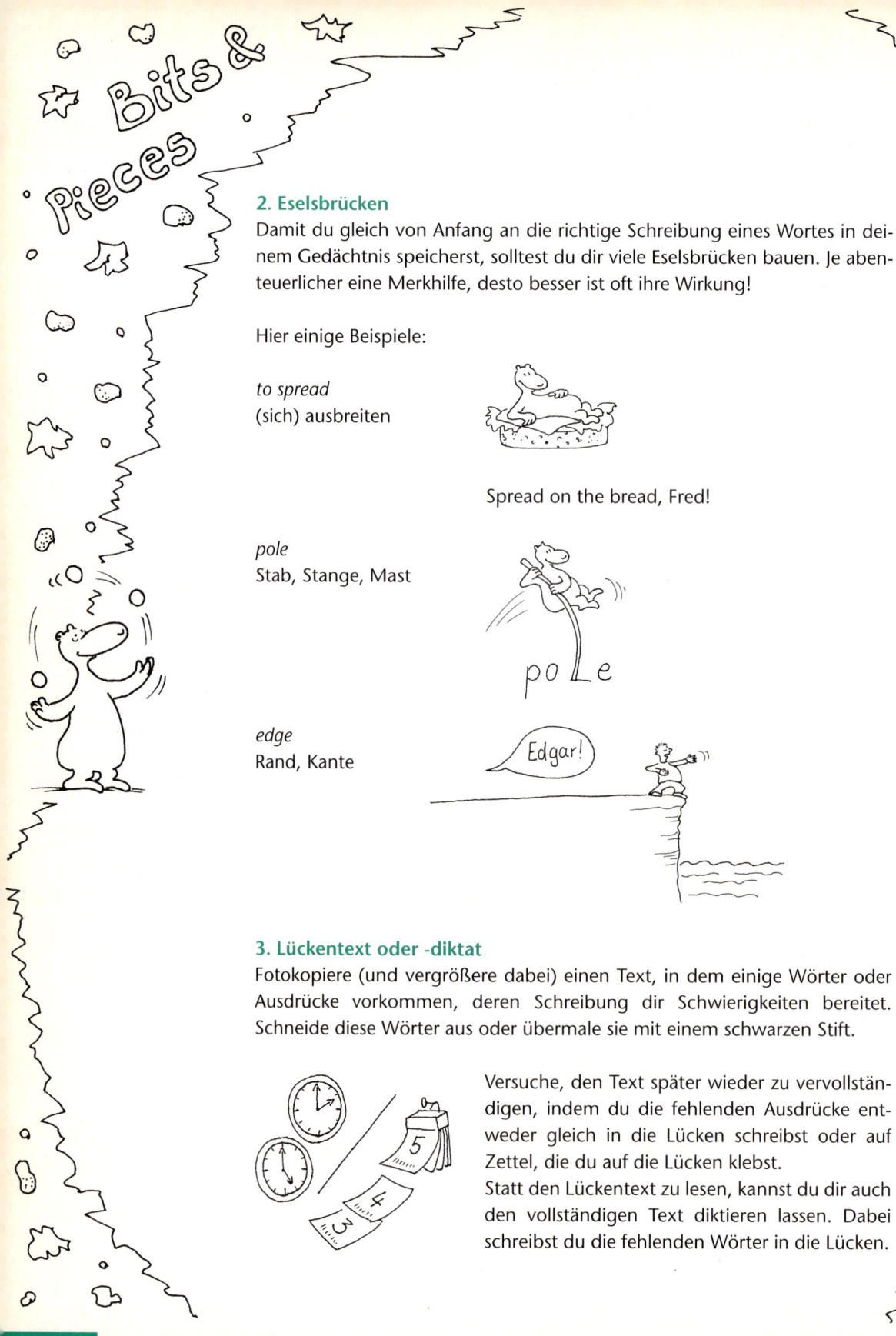

Damit du gleich von Anfang an die richtige Schreibung eines Wortes in deinem Gedächtnis speicherst, solltest du dir viele Eselsbrücken bauen. Je abenteuerlicher eine Merkhilfe, desto besser ist oft ihre Wirkung!

Hier einige Beispiele:

to spread
(sich) ausbreiten

Spread on the bread, Fred!

pole
Stab, Stange, Mast

edge
Rand, Kante

3. Lückentext oder -diktat

Fotokopiere (und vergrößere dabei) einen Text, in dem einige Wörter oder Ausdrücke vorkommen, deren Schreibung dir Schwierigkeiten bereitet. Schneide diese Wörter aus oder übermale sie mit einem schwarzen Stift.

Versuche, den Text später wieder zu vervollständigen, indem du die fehlenden Ausdrücke entweder gleich in die Lücken schreibst oder auf Zettel, die du auf die Lücken klebst.

Statt den Lückentext zu lesen, kannst du dir auch den vollständigen Text diktieren lassen. Dabei schreibst du die fehlenden Wörter in die Lücken.

Der Genitiv
The genitive

SECOND FLOOR
Men's Wear

FIRST FLOOR
Children's Wear
Teenagers' Corner

GROUND FLOOR
Ladies' Wear

Fred's new T-shirt

In diesem Kapitel erfährst du alles Wichtige über den „Besitzfall".

Der Genitiv oder „Besitzfall" wird gebraucht, wenn es um Besitz im weitesten Sinne geht. Oft haben wir es im Englischen mit einem *s*-Genitiv zu tun. Dabei wird an das betreffende Wort ein Apostroph und dann ein *s* angehängt. Manchmal steht der Apostroph aber auch nach dem *s*. Das klingt verwirrend, ist aber eigentlich ganz logisch. Es gibt nämlich eindeutige Regeln dafür – und genau diese Regeln wollen wir dir jetzt vorstellen.

1. Der *s*-Genitiv

's

Fred's new T-shirt

Freds neues T-Shirt

Mrs Bates's favourite hat
or: *Mrs Bates' favourite hat*

der Lieblingshut von Frau Bates

the girl's shoes

die Schuhe des Mädchens

Regel

Bei **Personen im Singular** (auch bei Namen, die auf *-s* enden) fügst du ein *'s* an.

the dog's bone
der Knochen
des Hundes

the dog's bones
die Knochen
des Hundes

Regel

Auch bei **Tieren im Singular** kannst du -'s anfügen.

men's wear
Herrenbekleidung

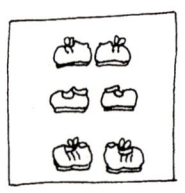

children's shoes
Kinderschuhe

Regel

Auch bei **unregelmäßigen Pluralformen** steht -'s.

Australia's wildlife
Australiens wild lebende Tiere

an hour's drive
eine einstündige Fahrt

Regel

Bei **Orts- und Ländernamen** kann -'s oder der *of*-Genitiv stehen. Verwende den *s*-Genitiv (-'s) auch bei **Zeitangaben im Singular**.

Na, das kannst du gleich mal üben!

Übersetze:

1. Barbaras Bruder
2. das Nest des Vogels
3. der neue Präsident von Kanada
4. die Füße des Jungen
5. Männersocken
6. der Kopf des Schweins
7. eine einstündige Pause
8. Kinderspielsachen
9. die größte Stadt Deutschlands
10. der Hund unserer Nachbarin

Exercise 11

Schauen wir uns nun die zweite Variante des s-Genitivs an: Es wird ein Apostroph an das bereits vorhandene s angehängt.

s'

girls' shoes	the Bakers' dogs	the dogs' bone	the dogs' bones
Mädchen-schuhe	die Hunde der Bakers	der Knochen der Hunde	die Knochen der Hunde

Regel

Bei **Personen und Tieren im Plural** wird bei **regelmäßiger Pluralform (-s)** ein **einfacher Apostroph** hinzugefügt.

Genitiv 131

a three hours' drive
eine dreistündige Fahrt

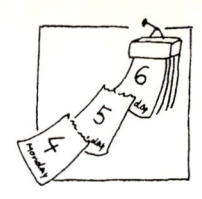

in two days' time
in zwei Tagen

Regel

Bei **Zeitangaben im Plural** steht ebenfalls *-s'*.

Auch hierzu eine kleine Übung:

Exercise 12

1 **delay**

1. das neue Auto der Millers ....
2. die Ohren der Pferde ....
3. die Jacken der Zwillinge ....
4. eine zweistündige Verspätung[1] ....
5. Hundekekse ....
6. das Zimmer meiner Eltern ....
7. der Garten der Greens ....
8. eine vierstündige Fahrt ....
9. die Fahrräder meiner Schwestern ....
10. die Ohren der Kaninchen ....

Es gibt aber noch eine zweite Form des Genitivs – den so genannten *of*-Genitiv. Wann sollst du diese Form verwenden?

2. Der *of*-Genitiv

of

the name of the game
der Name des Spiels

the colour of his hair
die Farbe seiner Haare

Regel

Bei **Dingen** verwendest du den *of*-Genitiv.

*the shoes of the guy
who thinks he's John Wayne*
die Schuhe des Typen,
der sich für John Wayne hält

*the name of the lady
who lives next door*
der Name der Dame,
die nebenan wohnt

Regel

Der *of*-Genitiv steht dann bei **Personen**, wenn eine **längere Erläuterung** folgt.

1. der Name der Straße ....
2. die Dächer der Häuser ....
3. die Wurzeln der Bäume ....
4. das Auto der Leute, die letzte Woche hier eingezogen sind ....
5. die Farbe meines neuen Regenschirms ....
6. die Namen der Tiere, die in Australien leben ....

Exercise 13

Genitiv

3. Der Genitiv ohne nachfolgendes Substantiv

Whose socks are these?

They are Fred's.

Nicht immer steht der Genitiv mit einem nachfolgenden Substantiv (Hauptwort). Besonders in der gesprochenen Sprache wird es oft weggelassen.

Is this book Kevin's?
No, it's Jane's.
Gehört das Buch Kevin?
Nein, es gehört Jane.

This ball isn't mine.
Is it yours?
Dieser Ball gehört nicht mir.
Ist es deiner?

Regel

Das nachfolgende **Substantiv kann entfallen**, wenn klar ist, worauf sich der Genitiv bezieht.

THIS WALL ISN'T MINE. Is it yours? Or is it his or hers? It's not ours. And it's not yours. MAYBE IT'S THEIRS!

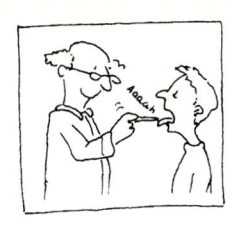

I went to the doctor's this morning.
Ich bin heute morgen zum Arzt gegangen.

I'm going to spend the weekend at my aunt's.
Ich verbringe das Wochenende bei meiner Tante.

> **Regel**
>
> Auch bei **Geschäften**, **Ärzten** und **Privathäusern** fällt meist das entsprechende Substantiv *(shop, surgery, house, flat)* weg.

Alles klar? Die nächste Übung wartet auf dich.

Mrs Silverstone hat immer einen vollen Terminkalender. Übersetze, was sie so alles macht.

Exercise 14

Am Montagmorgen ging sie zum Bäcker und zum Metzger.

....

....

Am Nachmittag war sie beim Zahnarzt und in der Apotheke.

....

....

Sie verbrachte den Dienstagvormittag beim Friseur.

....

....

Eine Dame fragte: „Ist der rote Sportwagen[1] ihrer?"
Mrs Silverstone antwortete: „Nein, das ist nicht meiner, er gehört meinem Bruder."

1 *Sportwagen* = **sports car**

....

....

....

Von Mittwoch bis Samstag blieb sie bei ihrer Schwester.

....

....

Genitiv 135

4. Der „doppelte" Genitiv

Zum Schluss noch eine Besonderheit: Ein *of*-Genitiv und ein *s*-Genitiv bzw. ein Possessivpronomen (besitzanzeigendes Fürwort) können auch miteinander kombiniert werden.

a friend of mine
ein Freund von mir

a friend of my father's
ein Freund meines Vaters

Regel

Der „doppelte" Genitiv macht deutlich, dass die jeweilige Person **mehrere** Freunde hat.
Man könnte auch sagen: *one of my friends, one of my father's friends*

Jetzt versuche es selbst.

Fred blättert in seinem Fotoalbum.

Exercise 15

Vervollständige die Sätze:

1. Das ist Julie, eine Freundin von mir aus Australien.

   That's Julie, _____ from Australia.

2. Das ist Pete. Ein Nachbar von ihm gießt gerade die Blumen.

   That's Pete. _____ is watering the flowers.

3. Charlies Onkel ist Feuerwehrmann. Das ist Charlie mit einigen Kollegen seines Onkels.

   Charlie's uncle is a fireman. That's Charlie with some colleagues _____

4. Und das ist Maggie. Jonglieren ist ein großes Hobby von ihr.

   And that's Maggie. Juggling is a great hobby _____

136 Genitiv

Bevor du dich an den Abschlusstest wagst, kannst du jetzt noch einmal überprüfen, ob alles „sitzt". In der folgenden Übung kommen alle Genitivformen vor.

Form sentences with the words – and use the correct form of the genitive. Be careful – the parts of the sentences are not in the right order!

1. the Millers/has got seats/new car/for seven people.

2. my room/are decorated/the walls/with lots of posters.

3. celebrated/a friend/his birthday/of mine/last Saturday.

4. brother/broke his leg/Linda/yesterday.

5. a/we have/break/twenty minutes/at 10.30.

6. the roof/has to be repaired/our neighbours/house.

7. the lady/is that/the purse/with the two poodles?

8. not/Jane/jacket/that's/it's/Diana.

9. clothes/are rather expensive/children/in this shop.

10. feathers/were glittering/the birds/in the sun.

11. had to go/to the dentist/my sister/this morning.

12. the Empire State Building/America/is/highest skyscrapers/one of.

Exercise 16

Test

(Je 2 Punkte für jeden richtig übersetzten Ausdruck)

Complete the following sentences:

1. Birgit is going to Australia as an au-pair girl _____ (in drei Wochen).

2. (Der Cousin ihres Vaters) _____ lives in Melbourne with his wife and their two daughters.

3. Birgit will have to look after the kids and _____ (die Hunde der Mädchen).

4. She has already seen _____ (ein Foto des Hauses) with the two girls sitting on the doorstep.

5. (Der Name des Mädchens) _____ with the long black hair is Mary-Ann,

6. and _____ (der Name ihrer Schwester) is Catherine.

7. It's _____ (ein zwanzigstündiger Flug) to Australia, and Birgit is a little afraid because she has never been so far away from home before.

8. (Eine Freundin von ihr) _____ promised Birgit that she would write her a letter every week.

9. (Beim Arzt) _____ Birgit read an interesting article in a magazine.

10. It was about _____ (die Tierwelt Australiens). Birgit likes kangaroos, and she is looking forward to seeing lots of them in the Australian outback.

Genitiv

Testauswertung

My personal scoreboard:

20–15 "right" scores:
There is only one thing to say:

14–10 "right" scores:
You got most of the 's, s' and of-genitives right.
Some of the forms are a little tricky. Which were the ones you had problems with? Have another look at these parts of this chapter.

9–0 "right" scores:
What went wrong? Maybe you didn't read the German expressions carefully enough. Or you did the test without having done all the exercises in this chapter?!

Von der Kunst, Wörter zu lernen ...

... und sie nicht wieder zu vergessen

Hast du dich auch schon oft geärgert, weil dir Wörter, die du wirklich gut gelernt hattest, am nächsten Tag schon nicht mehr einfielen? Keine Sorge – du leidest nicht an unheilbarer Vergesslichkeit, sondern dein Gedächtnis hatte einfach keine Chance, die neuen Vokabeln zu speichern. Mit der richtigen Technik ist das alles kein Problem! Die folgenden Tipps sollen dir dabei helfen. Du wirst staunen, zu welchen Leistungen dein Gedächtnis fähig ist!

Lerntipps

Tipps für das Wörterlernen

Tipp 1:

Eselsbrücken und Bilder im Kopf!

Es ist oft mühsam, sich einzelne Wörter zu merken. Bringt man sie dann mit einem Bild in Verbindung, stellt man fest, dass sie viel leichter im Gedächtnis haften bleiben. Diese Tatsache solltest du dir beim Vokabellernen zunutze machen.

Wenn du dir ein Wort einprägen willst, baue dir eine Eselsbrücke oder stelle dir ein Bild oder eine Situation vor. Je witziger und ausgefallener die Eselsbrücke ist, desto besser der Lernerfolg!

Auch der Klang eines Wortes kann eine solche Hilfe sein. Sprich die Wörter oder Ausdrücke immer laut vor dich hin, damit sich die Aussprache einprägt.

Hier einige Beispiele aus diesem Buch:

to spread
(sich) ausbreiten

Spread on the bread, Fred!

pole
Stab, Stange, Mast

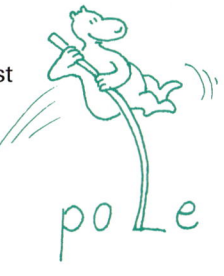

Man könnte meinen, dass zusätzliche Informationen das Gehirn nur unnötig belasten. Aber genau das Gegenteil ist hier der Fall. Die Eselsbrücken und anderen Gedächtnisstützen funktionieren wie zusätzliche Halteseile, mit denen das Wort im Netzwerk des Gedächtnisses verankert wird.

Lerntipps

Tipp 2:

Verbinde Unbekanntes mit Bekanntem!

Ein neues Wort ist gleich nicht mehr so allein, wenn es nette Gesellschaft in Form von bereits bekannten Wörtern bekommt. Und so verbindest du unbekannte Wörter mit solchen, die du bereits früher gelernt hast:

Du kennst das Gegenteil:

expensive	↔	cheap
boring	↔	interesting
difficult	↔	easy

Du kennst ein Wort aus der Wortfamilie:

| birthplace | → | birthday |
| familiar | → | family |

Du kennst bereits mehrere Wörter aus dem Wortfeld:

| peas | → | carrots, onions, beans |
| cheerful | → | friendly, nice, polite |

Zeichne zu jedem Wortfeld eine so genannte **Mind Map**. Du kannst die Skizze erweitern oder umgestalten, wenn ein neues Wort dazukommt.

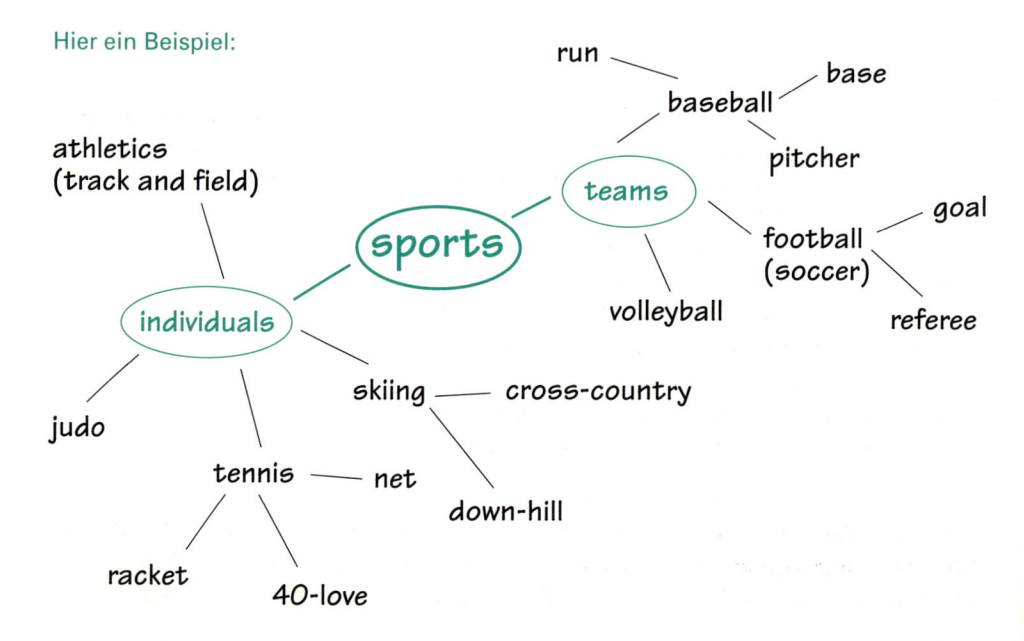

Hier ein Beispiel:

sports
- athletics (track and field)
- individuals
  - judo
  - tennis — net
    - racket
    - 40-love
  - skiing — cross-country
  - down-hill
- teams
  - baseball — run, base, pitcher
  - volleyball
  - football (soccer) — goal, referee

Tipp 3:

Auf die richtige Dosierung kommt es an!

Lerne nie mehr als 8–10 neue Vokabeln auf einmal! Du überforderst sonst dein Kurzzeitgedächtnis! Versuchst du, mehr zu „pauken", überschreibt dein Gedächtnis die zuerst gelernten Wörter, und du musst sie dir erneut einprägen.

Wiederhole diese 8–10 neu gelernten Wörter nach einer kurzen Pause (siehe Tipp 5). Danach solltest du etwas ganz anderes tun, z. B. Mathematik-Aufgaben lösen oder Flöte spielen. Wenn du an diesem Tag mehr als 10 neue Wörter lernen willst oder musst, kannst du dir die zweite Portion nach dieser Unterbrechung vornehmen – aber wieder nur 8–10 neue Vokabeln am Stück.

Wenn du dafür sorgst, dass die einzelnen Lernportionen überschaubar bleiben, dass möglichst nicht ähnliche Fächer (z. B. Englisch und Französisch) gleich aufeinander folgen und dass sich schriftliche und mündliche Tätigkeiten abwechseln, wird das Lernen für dich zum Kinderspiel!

Tipp 4:

Benutze mehrere Lernkanäle!

Nicht nur das Sehen, d. h. die bildliche Vorstellung, hilft dir beim Wörterlernen. Auch über das Hören, das Fühlen und die Bewegung kannst du Informationen besser im Gedächtnis verankern. Mit Hilfe eines Kassettenrekorders lassen sich neue Wörter hervorragend lernen und wiederholen. Sprich die englischen Wörter oder auch kurze Sätze auf eine leere Kassette und lass genügend lange Pausen dazwischen. Beim Abspielen ergänzt du in diesen Pausen die deutschen Begriffe. Im Anschluss daran sprichst du die deutschen Wörter auf Band und ergänzt beim Abspielen die englischen Entsprechungen.

Vielleicht hilft es dir, beim Wörterlernen im Zimmer auf und ab zu gehen oder mit deinen Händen Gesten oder Zeichnungen in der Luft zu vollführen. Beim Lernen mit Karteikärtchen kannst du den Tastsinn mit einbeziehen. Viele Anregungen zu Wörterdominos und anderen Spielen findest du in **Keep it up! 2.**

Tipps gegen das Vergessen

Tipp 5:

Ohne Wiederholen geht es nicht!

Dein Kurzzeitgedächtnis kann neue Informationen nur für einen begrenzten Zeitraum speichern. Deshalb vergisst du vieles, was du nur einmal gelesen oder gehört hast, ganz schnell wieder. Um die entsprechenden Daten vom Kurzzeitspeicher ins Langzeitgedächtnis zu befördern, hilft nur eines: wiederholen!

Wenn du am Nachmittag neue Wörter gelernt hast (so wie in den Tipps 1 – 4 empfohlen), solltest du sie dir am Abend, also nach einigen Stunden, noch einmal vornehmen. Dein Gedächtnis braucht diese Unterstützung, um das Gelernte sicher und langfristig zu speichern. Dann kann es auch nicht passieren, dass du am nächsten Tag in der Englischstunde abgefragt wirst und die Hälfte der Wörter schon nicht mehr weißt, obwohl du sie doch „gelernt" hast. Nach etwa 4 – 5 Wiederholungsrunden – dazu zählt auch die Verwendung der entsprechenden Vokabeln im Unterricht – ist ein Wort oder Ausdruck dann relativ sicher im Langzeitgedächtnis gespeichert und kann jederzeit abgerufen werden. Das Wiederholen lohnt sich also auf jeden Fall!

Tipp 6:

Verwende die Wörter auf verschiedene Arten!

Das sture Herunterleiern von Vokabellisten ist nicht unbedingt eine geeignete Art der Wiederholung. Viel sinnvoller ist es, wenn du versuchst, die gelernten Wörter bei der Wiederholung am Abend anzuwenden.

Du könntest zum Beispiel eine Geschichte aus dem Lehrbuch anhand der neu gelernten Wörter nacherzählen. Oder du suchst dir jeweils zwei Wörter aus und machst daraus einen Satz. Sprich dabei laut (oder auch leise) vor dich hin. Wenn du gerne malst oder zeichnest, kannst du ein Bild mit den neuen Wörter beschriften oder eine *Mind Map* gestalten. Du wirst bald merken, dass sich auf diese Weise nicht nur deine Wortschatzkenntnisse deutlich verbessern!

Lerntipps

Tipp 7:

Vokabelkartei

Besser als ein Vokabelheft eignet sich die Vokabelkartei zum Wörterlernen. Denn die Karteikärtchen lassen sich mischen und immer wieder neu ordnen, während die Wörter im Vokabelheft immer in der gleichen Reihenfolge stehen. Du kannst dir deinen Karteikasten aus einem Schuhkarton selbst basteln.

Klebe vier Trennwände ein, sodass fünf unterschiedlich große Fächer entstehen. Das erste Fach ist das kleinste, das fünfte Fach das größte. Die einzelnen Karteikarten schneidest du aus etwas festerem Papier zu, indem du ein DIN-A4-Blatt so lange immer wieder halbierst, bis kleine Karten entstanden sind.

Beschrifte die Kärtchen auf beiden Seiten.

Vorderseite:

(sich) ausleihen, borgen

Kann ich mir dein Skateboard ausleihen?

Rückseite:

to borrow

Can I borrow your skateboard?

Zunächst stecken alle neu zu lernenden Wörter im ersten Fach. Wenn du ein Wort gewusst hast, wandert es ins zweite Fach. Wiederholst du nach einiger Zeit die Wörter im zweiten Fach, wandern diejenigen, die du immer noch weißt, ins dritte Fach. Die anderen, die du nicht mehr weißt, müssen zurück ins erste Fach. Jedes Wort, das auf diese Weise ein Fach weiterwandert, bringt ein kleines Erfolgserlebnis. Sind die Wörter im fünften und letzten Fach angelangt, kannst du sie nach einiger Zeit aussortieren, denn sie sind jetzt auch in deinem Langzeitgedächtnis gespeichert.

Dieses Verfahren eignet sich besonders für Wörter, die du dir nicht so leicht merken kannst.

Viel Spaß und Erfolg beim Wörterlernen!

Lerntipps

Quellenverzeichnis

Seite	Quelle
37	Aus: Langenscheidt's Power Dictionary, Englisch – Deutsch und Deutsch – Englisch, Berlin, München, 1997, S. 583f.
86	Aus: Langenscheidt's Power Dictionary, Englisch – Deutsch und Deutsch – Englisch, Berlin, München, 1997, S. 54

Stichwortverzeichnis

f. bedeutet: Du findest das Stichwort auf der angegebenen und der folgenden Seite.
ff. bedeutet: Du findest das Stichwort auf der angegebenen und mehreren folgenden Seiten.
B & P bedeutet: *Bits & Pieces*

B

Bilder beschriften B & P 18f.

F

Fragen und Antworten *(Questions and Answers)* 20ff.
    Bitten, Einladungen, Vorschläge 22ff.
    Entscheidungsfragen *(Yes/No Questions)* 27ff.
    Fragen mit Fragepronomen 29ff.

G

Genitiv *(Genitive)* 129ff.
    doppelter Genitiv 136f.
    ohne nachfolgendes Substantiv 134f.
    of-Genitiv 133, 137
    s-Genitiv 129ff., 137
Gespräche führen 20ff.

H

Hören und Sprechen B & P 57f.

I

Indirekte Rede *(Reported Speech)* 76ff., 114ff.
    Aussagesätze 76ff.
    Befehlssätze 120ff.
    Fragesätze 115ff., 123f.
    Zeitenfolge 78ff., 114f.

K

Kurzantworten *(Question Tags)* 27, 29

L

Lerntechniken B & P 18f., 37f., 57f., 74f., 86f., 96f., 112f., 127f.
Lesen *(Reading)* B & P 96f.

M

Meinungsäußerungen 32ff.

P

Passiv *(Passive)* 98ff.
    Aktiv und Passiv 103ff.
    in Verbindung mit *can, must* und *may* 106f.
    persönliches Passiv 108f.
    Zeitformen 99ff., 110

R

Rechtschreibung *(Spelling)* B & P 127f.

S

Sprechen *(Talking)* 20f., B & P 74f.

T

Telefonieren *(Telephoning)* 25f.

U

Unbestimmte Pronomen 88ff.
    each – every 91f.
    (a) little – (a) few 93f.
    much – many – a lot (of) 92f.
    some – any 88ff.
Unregelmäßige Verben *(Irregular Verbs)* 10, B & P 112f.
Unvollständige Hilfsverben *(Defective Auxiliaries)* 59ff., 70ff.
    can und Ersatzformen 59ff., 70f.
    may und Ersatzformen 62f., 70f.
    must und Ersatzformen 64ff., 70f.

V

Verlaufsform *(Progressive Form)* 39f., 48f., 53f.

W

Wörterbuch *(Dictionary)* B & P 37f., B & P 86f.
Wörter lernen B & P 18f., 112f., 128f.

Z

Zeiten *(Tenses)* 7ff., 39ff.
    Bildung der Zeiten 7ff.
    Present Perfect mit *since* und *for* 50ff.
    Simple Past und *Past Progressive* 48f.
    Simple Past und *Present Perfect* 40ff.

MENTOR LERN-HILFE

Band 545

Englisch

7./8. Klasse

Keep it up! 1

Ein Übungsprogramm für Grammatik und Wortschatz 1

Lösungsteil
(an der Perforation abtrennen)

Astrid Stannat
Dieter D'Zenit
Willi Mey

mentor Verlag München

Lösungen Kapitel A

Exercise A 1
S. 9

Simple Past

regelmäßige Verben:
-ed an die Grundform
unregelmäßige Verben:
2. Form

Future I

will + Grundform
des Verbs
im Mündlichen:
'll + Grundform

Simple Present

Grundform des Verbs
3. Pers. Singular *(he, she, it)*:
-s wird angehängt

Past Perfect

had + 3. Form
    (*-ed* oder
    (unregelm. Form)

Present Perfect

I, you, we, they have + 3. Form
he, she, it   *has* + 3. Form

Exercise A 2
S. 10

gehen:	go – went – gone
liegen:	lie – lay – lain
vergessen:	forget – forgot – forgotten
schreiben:	write – wrote – written
ziehen:	draw – drew – drawn
werfen:	throw – threw – thrown
wissen:	know – knew – known
singen:	sing – sang – sung
trinken:	drink – drank – drunk
geben:	give – gave – given
essen:	eat – ate – eaten
fallen:	fall – fell – fallen

Exercise A 3
S. 11

Past Perfect	Simple Past	Present Perfect	Simple Present	Future
he had played	he played	he has played	he plays	he will play
she had gone	she went	she has gone	she goes	she will go
I had opened	I opened	I have opened	I open	I will open
we had come	we came	we have come	we come	we will come
I had tried	I tried	I have tried	I try	I will try
he had written	he wrote	he has written	he writes	he will write
she had seen	she saw	she has seen	she sees	she will see
they had spent	they spent	they have spent	they spend	they will spend
she had read	she read	she has read	she reads	she will read
it had rained	it rained	it has rained	it rains	it will rain

Exercise A 4
S. 11f.

When I've woken up, I get up.
When I've got up, I wash.
When I've washed, I put on my clothes.
When I've put on my clothes, I go downstairs into the kitchen.
When I've gone downstairs into the kitchen, I have breakfast.
When I've had breakfast, I go into the garden.
When I've gone into the garden, I play football.
When I've played football, I read a book.
When I've read a book, I write a letter.
When I've written a letter, I buy a pound of apples.
When I've bought a pound of apples, I feed the horses.

Fortsetzung Exercise A 4
S. 11f.

When I've fed the horses, I draw a picture.
When I've drawn a picture, I sing a song.
When I've sung a song, I repair the car.
When I've repaired the car, I tell a story.
When I've told a story, I watch TV.
When I've watched TV, I go to bed.

When he has woken up, he gets up.
When he has got up, he washes.
When he has washed, he puts on his clothes.
When he has put on his clothes, he goes downstairs into the kitchen.
When he has gone downstairs into the kitchen, he has breakfast.
When he has had breakfast, he goes into the garden.
When he has gone into the garden, he plays football.
When he has played football, he reads a book.
When he has read a book, he writes a letter.
When he has written a letter, he buys a pound of apples.
When he has bought a pound of apples, he feeds the horses.
When he has fed the horses, he draws a picture.
When he has drawn a picture, he sings a song.
When he has sung a song, he repairs the car.
When he has repaired the car, he tells a story.
When he has told a story, he watches TV.
When he has watched TV, he goes to bed.

Exercise A 5
S. 13

Past Perfect	Simple Past	Present Perfect	Simple Present	Future
we hadn't known	we didn't know	we haven't known	we don't know	we won't know
it hadn't helped	it didn't help	it hasn't helped	it doesn't help	it won't help
she hadn't given	she didn't give	she hasn't given	she doesn't give	she won't give
you hadn't won	you didn't win	you haven't won	you don't win	you won't win
I hadn't moved	I didn't move	I haven't moved	I don't move	I won't move
he hadn't forgotten	he didn't forget	he hasn't forgotten	he doesn't forget	he won't forget
they hadn't bought	they didn't buy	they haven't bought	they don't buy	they won't buy
we hadn't seen	we didn't see	we haven't seen	we don't see	we won't see
she hadn't spent	she didn't spend	she hasn't spent	she doesn't spend	she won't spend
I hadn't slept	I didn't sleep	I haven't slept	I don't sleep	I won't sleep

Past Perfect	Simple Past	Present Perfect	Simple Present	Future	Exercise A 6
had he liked?	did he like?	has he liked?	does he like?	will he like?	S. 14
had you caught?	did you catch?	have you caught?	do you catch?	will you catch?	
had he forgotten?	did he forget?	has he forgotten?	does he forget?	will he forget?	
had they gone?	did they go?	have they gone?	do they go?	will they go?	
had we hit?	did we hit?	have we hit?	do we hit?	will we hit?	
had they seen?	did they see?	have they seen?	do they see?	will they see?	
had you told?	did you tell?	have you told?	do you tell?	will you tell?	
had I opened?	did I open?	have I opened?	do I open?	will I open?	
had he taken?	did he take?	has he taken?	does he take?	will he take?	
had she lost?	did she lose?	has she lost?	does she lose?	will she lose?	

Exercise A 7
S. 15

Hier einige weitere Vorschläge:

I didn't move: The bear was only about twenty metres away from me. I didn't move. …

it will rain: Our neighbour is washing his car. I'm pretty sure it will rain in the afternoon. It always rains after he has washed his car.

do you catch? You always go fishing at the weekends. Do you ever catch any fish – or do you just go fishing for the fun of it?

Test
S. 15 f.

nehmen:	take	took	taken
verstecken:	hide	hid	hidden
wissen:	know	knew	known
lesen:	read	read	read
fallen:	fall	fell	fallen
machen:	make	made	made
bauen:	build	built	built
erzählen:	tell	told	told
kaufen:	buy	bought	bought
fühlen:	feel	felt	felt

We will arrive at the airport in time.
Judy gets up at five o'clock every day.
The Greens haven't sold their car.
Brian doesn't have pancakes for breakfast every day.
Had they met before?
Janet bought that dress in New York.

Pictures and Words

Bits & Pieces
S. 18 f.

Folgende Autoteile solltest du kennzeichnen:

windscreen – *Windschutzscheibe*
mudguard – *Kotflügel*
steering wheel – *Lenkrad*
bumper – *Stoßstange*
boot – *Kofferraum*
rear lights – *Rücklichter*

front lights – *vordere Scheinwerfer*
petrol tank – *Tank*
number plate – *Nummernschild*
bonnet – *Motorhaube*
tyre – *Reifen*
windscreen wipers – *Scheibenwischer*

Lösungen Kapitel B

Exercise B 1
S. 20

What's your name?	My name is Fred.
What are your hobbies?	I like reading, swimming, and waterskiing.
Are you good at school?	Well, I'm quite good at languages, but maths isn't my cup of tea!
I'm from Adelaide. That's in the south of Australia.	Where are you from?
The "Spice Girls" are my favourite group but I also like Australian bands like "Men at Work".	What kind of music do you like?
I'm fourteen.	How old are you?
You mean that traditional Aborigine instrument? No, I'm afraid I can't.	Can you play the didgeridoo?

Exercise B 2
S. 21

Wenn du wissen möchtest, ob das Mädchen oder der Junge   *dann müsstest du fragen:*

1. eine(n) Brieffreund(in) hat,	Have you got a pen-friend?
2. gerne Reisen unternimmt,	Do you like travelling?
3. schon mal in Deutschland war,	Have you ever been to Germany?
5. eine gute Sportlerin/ein guter Sportler ist,	Are you good at sports?
5. ein Haustier hat,	Have you got a pet?
6. in einer großen Stadt wohnt,	Do you live in a big city?
7. gerne Techno-Musik hört,	Do you like listening to Techno music?
8. Geschwister hat,	Have you got any brothers or sisters?
9. am Nachmittag Schule hat,	Have you got school in the afternoon?
10. schon mal die Schule geschwänzt hat,	Have you ever played truant?
11. mit dir zum Strand gehen will,	Would you like to go to the beach with me?
12. mit dir in Verbindung bleiben möchte.	Would you like to keep in touch with me?

Exercise B 3
S. 24

Die folgenden Sätze stellen jeweils nur eine von mehreren Möglichkeiten dar. Vielleicht hast du eine andere Formulierung gewählt:

1. Would you like to come to my birthday party?
2. Do you think you could lend me your air matress?
3. How about spending our next holiday in Ireland?
4. Could you pass me the salt, please?
5. Let's go to the hotel disco tonight!
6. We'd be very pleased if you and your parents came to dinner next Friday.

Exercise B 4
S. 25 f.

Hello, Mrs Winkler!
This is Fred speaking.
Can I talk to Jörg?

Hello, Fred. I'll go and get him.
Hold on!

Thank you.

Hello, Fred. It's Jörg here.

Hello, Jörg. How are you?

I'm fine, thanks. And you?

I'm alright. Listen, Jörg. We are planning to have a barbecue next Saturday. I'd like you to come, too. Are you free on Saturday evening?

Oh Fred, could you speak a little more slowly, please? Well, I have a football match on Saturday.

Oh, what a pity!
At what time is the match?

At five o'clock.

You could come after the match, couldn't you?

Yes, if that's o. k. with you.

That's great! I hope your team will win. I'll keep my fingers crossed for you!

Thank you, Fred! I'm sure that'll help! Thanks for ringing and see you on Saturday, then!

See you on Saturday. Bye!

Hier ist …/Hier spricht …   a) This is … speaking.
　　　　　　　　　　　　　　b) It's … here.

Kann ich … sprechen?   Can I talk to …?

Bleib dran!   Hold on!

Könntest du bitte etwas langsamer sprechen?   Could you speak a little more slowly, please?

Wie geht's dir?   How are you?

Mir geht's gut.   a) I'm fine, thanks.
　　　　　　　　b) I'm alright.

Hast du am Samstag Zeit?   Are you free on Saturday?

Danke, dass du angerufen hast.   Thanks for ringing.

Bis Samstag!   See you on Saturday!

Exercise B 5
S. 27

Do you understand me?　　　　　　　　Yes, I do.
May/Can I ask you some questions?　　Yes, you may/can.
Are you from Mars?　　　　　　　　　　No, I'm not.
Did you come by spacecraft?　　　　　　No, I didn't.
Do your parents know where you are?　Yes, they do.
Have you got any friends here?　　　　　Yes, I have.
Would you like something to eat?　　　　No, thank you.
Could you please tell me something
about your planet?　　　　　　　　　　　Yes, of course.
Will you go back to your planet soon?　　No, I won't.

Lösungen

Exercise B 6
S. 28
1. Does Jack live in London?
2. Did I lock the door last night?
3. Does your brother speak Italian?
4. Did you go out last Saturday?
5. Did the Millers spend their holidays in Florida last year?
6. Do you always get up so early?
7. Do your parents like dogs?
8. Did Jenny do well in her last English test?

Exercise B 7
S. 30
Who is that man? – Charles Breakneck!
When did you last see him? – Last Friday.
Where was that? – In the Penguin Bar.
What was he wearing? – A coat, I think.
What coat? – A leather coat.
What colour? – Black.
How long did he stay there? – The whole evening, until one o'clock, I think.
How much money did he spend there? – I don't know, but I'm sure it was more than £ 100.
How many people were there that night? – Oh, it was quite crowded, more than 50, I think.
How often do you normally go there? – Twice a week.
Why do you go there? – I like the atmosphere. And I like to meet people.
Who do you meet there? – Friends.

Exercise B 8
S. 31
1. a) Who saw the two robbers at Victoria Station?
   b) Who did a fifteen-year-old boy see?

2. a) What hit my teacher on the head?
   b) Who did the apple hit on the head?

3. a) Who likes Mrs Brown?
   b) Who do all the pupils like?

4. a) Who often sees flying saucers in her garden?
   b) What does Helen often see in her garden?

5. a) Who loves Matthew?
   b) Who does Judith love?

6. a) Who followed the black limousine?
   b) What did the detective follow?

Exercise B 9
S. 32
Where do you live?
Where were you yesterday evening?
Who saw you there?
How long did you stay there?
Where is your car key?
Do you know the woman on the photo?
Where does she live?
When did you last see her?

Exercise B 10
S. 32
If you ask me – people watch too much television!
– I agree with you.

Lösungen

In my opinion all those sitcoms on TV are complete rubbish!
– Oh no, that's not true! I really enjoy watching "Roseanne".

When the weather is nice, I don't like sitting in front of the goggle-box.
– Neither do I!

I think there shouldn't be any commercials on TV.
– Well, of course, but on the other hand, you wouldn't want to have pay TV only, or would you?

Exercise B 11
S. 34

Hier einige Vorschläge:

It's good to learn a foreign language.
– I think so, too. When you go on holiday, you can talk to the people whose language you are learning.

Homework is necessary.
– O. K., only practice makes perfect. But on the other hand there is too much homework sometimes.

Girls shouldn't play football.
– That's rubbish! I don't agree at all! If a girl likes playing football, why on earth shouldn't she?

Exercise B 12
S. 35

1. In my opinion three months of school holidays are too long!
2. I don't think so!/I don't agree with you! Children and teenagers need this time to relax.
3. As far as I know, most pupils sleep during the lessons. I think that's enough!
4. I just can't agree with you!/I don't think so! A school day is really exhausting, and afterwards the pupils/students have to do their homework.
5. Rubbish! There's no school at the weekends, and there are holidays every few weeks. The kids just don't know what to do with their spare/free time.
6. That's not true. We simply need time for our family, our friends and our hobbies. I'm sure that you don't want to work every day, either!

Test
S. 36

(1.)
1. Are you American?
2. When do you get up in the morning?
3. Where do you live?
4. Could you please lend me your bike?
5. What did you do last Saturday?
6. Who wrote "Frankenstein"?
7. Have you ever been to Malta?
8. Where does your brother work?

(2.)
1. As far as I know, most school uniforms are dark blue, grey or dark green.
2. In my opinion/I think everybody should be able to decide for himself/herself what he/she wants to wear.
3. That's just what I think. If you ask me – school uniforms look boring.
4. Yes, but on the other hand the school is no disco! A lot of boys and girls spend hours in front of their wardrobe!
5. I agree with you completely! For many kids clothes are extremely important – too important!

Lösungen 157

Bits & Pieces
S. 37f.

Arbeit mit dem Wörterbuch

1. *Gangart:*	walk		5. *beim Essen:*	course
2. *Weg:*	way		6. *beim Auto:*	gear
3. *Flur:*	corridor		7. *Verlauf:*	course
4. *im Flugzeug:*	aisle			

Postkarte:	postcard
Landkarte:	map
Fahrkarte:	ticket
Speisekarte:	menu

Eisenbahn:	train
Schachzug:	move

Kochrezept:	recipe
Rezept v. Arzt:	prescription

Geldinstitut:	bank
Sitzbank:	bench, seat

Bild (allg.):	picture
Gemälde:	painting
Foto:	photo(graph)
Zeichnung:	drawing

B + C

Lösungen Kapitel C

Exercise C 1
S. 40

Past Perfect (Simple):	he had caught a dead whale
Past Perfect (Progressive):	which had been drifting
Past (Simple):	When he wanted to reel in …
	he got the shock of his life
	It took me about …
Past (Progressive):	Mr J. Gallagher … was fishing …
Present Perfect (Simple):	this is the biggest "fish" I've ever caught
Present Perfect (Progressive):	I've been going fishing for more than 15 years

Exercise C 2
S. 42

– Where <u>did you spend</u> your holidays?
– We <u>were</u> in Spain.
– <u>Was</u> it nice?
– Yes, it was. We <u>had</u> a nice holiday home near the beach. In the morning we often <u>visited</u> some sights and in the afternoon we <u>went</u> to the beach and <u>played</u> volleyball or <u>swam</u> in the sea.
– <u>Did you meet</u> any nice people?
– Yes, there <u>was</u> a family from Hamburg with two girls. One <u>was</u> 14, the other one <u>was</u> 12. We <u>did</u> a lot of things together.
– What <u>was</u> the food like?

Lösungen

- Most of the time we <u>cooked</u> our own meals. Every few days we <u>went</u> to a restaurant and <u>ate</u> some typical Spanish food. Only once I <u>had</u> something I <u>didn't like</u>. Apart from that it <u>was</u> always very tasty.
- By the way – many thanks for your postcard! I <u>got</u> it yesterday.
- Only yesterday? I <u>wrote</u> it more than two weeks ago!

Exercise C 3
S. 44f.

Oh, yes, we have often gone (been) there.
And we have already spent some weeks in New York.
Yes, we have also sailed across the Atlantic Ocean.
And we have flown to Japan.
Have you ever crossed the Sahara desert on the back of a camel?
No, we have never done that before. But we don't like the idea.
Have you ever climbed Mount Everest?
No, we haven't climbed it yet. But I think it's too dangerous.
We have already visited the Maoris in New Zealand!
No, we have never stayed at home. (No, we have never done that.)

Exercise C 4
S. 47

Have you ever eaten bacon and eggs?
Yes, I ate it on the boat last week.

Have you ever drunk English tea?
No, I haven't drunk it yet. Yesterday in London I had coffee.

Have you ever tasted grilled sausages?
I have often had them at home. But I have never tried them for breakfast.

Have you ever eaten sugar puffs?
Sugar puffs? No! I have never eaten them. But I would like to try them.

Exercise C 5
S. 48f.

I was having a shower
you were having a shower
he/she was having a shower

we were having a shower
you were having a shower
they were having a shower

Exercise C 6
S. 49

1. Tom and Judy were playing tennis.
2. The Johnsons were having a barbecue.
3. Fred was riding on his bike. (Fred was cycling.)
4. Mr Greenfield was washing his car.
5. Linda, Joan and Kevin were watching a film at the cinema.
6. Our neighbour's cat was sleeping on a (garden) chair.

Exercise C 7
S. 49

1. The pupils <u>were throwing</u> scraps of paper at each other when the teacher <u>came</u> in.
2. While the Barristers <u>were having</u> dinner, there <u>was</u> a knock at the door.
3. Sally <u>was eating</u> a banana when a monkey suddenly <u>jumped</u> on her shoulder.
4. The lights <u>went</u> out while we <u>were playing</u> cards.
5. While Sherlock Holmes, the famous detective, <u>was looking</u> at some pictures, he <u>had</u> an idea.
6. Fred <u>was reading</u> a ghost story when he suddenly <u>heard</u> footsteps.

Lösungen

Exercise C 8
S. 52
For three days.
For two hours.
Since last Tuesday.
Since yesterday.
For two weeks.

Exercise C 9
S. 52
Hier einige Möglichkeiten:

For two weeks.
Since my last birthday.
For three years.
For six months.
Since last Christmas.
…

Exercise C 10
S. 53
I have been waiting for him …
you have been waiting
he/she has been waiting
we have been waiting
you have been waiting
they have been waiting

Exercise C 11
S. 54
1. Mr Brown has been working in the garden since this morning.
2. Carol has been washing her car since five o'clock.
3. Ann has been watching TV for half an hour.
4. Tom's grandpa has been reading the newspaper since breakfast.
5. Susan has been writing a letter since she came home from school.
6. Mr Standish has been preparing the dinner for two hours.
7. Fred has been suffering from stomach-ache since he ate that lovely cake.
8. Tom and Peter have been playing chess for three hours.

Test
S. 56f.
1. We've been waiting here for two hours!
2. I've never been to the Tower of London (before) – and now it's closed!
3. Did you buy this hat at Portobello Market yesterday?
4. We were (just) going to the bus stop when it started to rain.
5. I have had this umbrella since I was in London in April.
6. He has been standing here since six o'clock!

Bits & Pieces
S. 58
Hören und Sprechen

d *oder* t?	bed	*Bett*	bet	*Wette, wetten*
	tie	*binden, Krawatte*	die	*sterben*
	tent	*Zelt*	tend	*neigen*

b *oder* p?	bath	*Bad*	path	*Pfad, Weg*
	pack	*packen*	back	*Rücken, zurück*
	pig	*Schwein*	big	*groß*

g *oder* c?	guard	*Wächter*	card	*Karte*
	coat	*Mantel*	goat	*Ziege*
	came	*kam*	game	*Spiel*

Lösungen

Lösungen Kapitel D

Exercise D 1
S. 59

He is able to walk without any help.
He is able to switch on the radio.
He is able to drink from a cup.
He is able to build a tower with his bricks.

Exercise D 2
S. 60

He couldn't walk without any help.
He couldn't switch on the radio.
He couldn't drink from a cup.
He couldn't build a tower with his bricks.
He wasn't able to walk without any help.
He wasn't able to switch on the radio.
He wasn't able to drink from a cup.
He wasn't able to build a tower with his bricks.

Exercise D 3
S. 61

1. My penfriend Fiona { can / is able to } speak a little German.
2. I { can't / 'm not allowed to } go to the concert with you …
3. The hippo { could / was able to } juggle with four balls.
4. … – he { can / is allowed to } go camping with us.
5. On the motorways you { couldn't / weren't allowed to } drive more than 70 mph.

Exercise D 4
S. 62

1. You { may / are allowed to } use this door only in case of emergency.
2. You { may not / are not allowed to } enter the road.
3. You { may not / are not allowed to } overtake cars, but you { may / are allowed to } overtake tractors.
4. You { may / are allowed to } bring your dog to the zoo, but you must keep it on the lead.
5. You { may not / are not allowed to } smoke here.

Exercise D 5
S. 63

We were allowed to listen to music in our rooms …
We weren't allowed to make any noise after ten.
There was a little lake nearby, but I wasn't allowed to go swimming there!
We were allowed to go to the public swimming-bath …
They had quite a number of bicycles and go-carts, and we were allowed to use them …
On the last day my friend Chris wanted to go shopping to the town centre. He wasn't allowed to go alone, so I went with him.

D

Exercise D 6
S. 64
First I have to do the shopping for her.
Then I have to fetch her some medicine from the chemist's.
After that I have to make her some tea.
And then I have to feed Tiffy, her cat.
When I come home I have to do my homework.

Exercise D 7
S. 64
She has to do the shopping for her.
Then she has to fetch her some medicine from the chemist's.
After that she has to make her some tea.
And then she has to feed Tiffy, her grandma's cat.
When she comes home, she has to do her homework.

Exercise D 8
S. 64
First we had to do the shopping.
Then we had to fetch some medicine from the chemist's.
After that we had to make Grandma some tea.
And then we had to feed Tiffy.
When I came home, I had to do my homework.

Exercise D 9
S. 66
I don't have to hurry to catch the bus.
I don't have to do any homework in the afternoon.
I don't have to write any tests.
I don't have to wear my school uniform.
I don't have to go to bed at eight.

I needn't hurry to catch the bus.
I needn't do any homework in the afternoon.
I needn't write any tests.
I needn't wear my school uniform.
I needn't go to bed at eight.

He doesn't have to hurry to catch the bus.
He doesn't have to do any homework in the afternoon.
He doesn't have to write any tests.
He doesn't have to wear his school uniform.
He doesn't have to go to bed at eight.

Exercise D 10
S. 67
You mustn't smoke too much.
I needn't/don't have to get up early tomorrow. There is no school.
You needn't/don't have to write Tom a letter, he will be here tomorrow.
But Margret, you mustn't hit your little brother!
Bob, you mustn't forget to answer Henry's letter.
Henry, you mustn't drink so much Coke.
You needn't/don't have to eat all that pudding if you are not hungry.
You mustn't forget to write to me soon.
You needn't/don't have to feed the dog. I've already done it.

Lösungen

Hier einige Möglichkeiten:

Last week Angie had to water the flowers. She also had to clear the table.
She didn't have to lay the table. And she didn't have to feed the rabbits, either.
On Sunday she had to go for a walk with Scruffy.

Chris had to go for a walk with Scruffy on Tuesday, Wednesday and Friday,
he didn't have to go on the other days.
Dad and Chris had to lay the table. They didn't have to clear the table.

Exercise D 11
S. 68

There is a small zoo in our town. Last week I <u>was allowed to</u> go there with my sister. My father <u>couldn't/wasn't able to</u> come with us, he <u>had to</u> work, so we <u>had to</u> take the bus. I <u>was allowed to</u> take my brother's camera with me but I <u>had to</u> promise him to be very careful.
When we reached the entrance we first <u>had to</u> buy the tickets. My sister <u>was allowed to</u> visit the zoo for half the price, as she is only eight years old. First we went to the monkeys. There was a sign: You <u>mustn't</u> feed the animals. The keeper told us that people who fed the monkeys <u>had to</u> pay a high fine.
My sister likes the hippopotamus very much. She was very happy when she <u>was allowed to</u> help the keeper to feed it. I <u>had to</u> take a picture of her in front of the pool. We <u>were allowed to</u> ride on the elephant that carries visitors through the zoo. At six o'clock we <u>had to</u> leave the zoo.

Exercise D 12
S. 69

they will be able to understand

we will have to speak
we won't have to speak

I will be allowed to send
I won't be allowed to send

Exercise D 13
S. 70

1. Will we be able to see Xenos from there?
2. No, you won't be able to see Xenos… But there will be a video call every ten days, and you will be able to see and talk to your family then.
3. Do you think we will have to stay inside the buildings all the time?
4. When it rains or snows, we will have to wear special clothes.
5. Will we have to go to school every day?
6. No. We will not have to go to school at the weekends…
7. Is it true that we will not be allowed to speak Xenophonic at school?
8. That's right. We will have to speak Earthian at school. But we will be allowed to meet once a week and speak our own language then.
9. I hope I will be able to play it…
10. I'm sure you will be allowed to join the school baseball team.

Exercise D 14
S. 71

1. … I wasn't allowed to go to school for a/one week.
2. Next year my brother will be able to swim.
3. You needn't/don't have to wait for me.
4. I couldn't/wasn't able to ride a bike at the age of six (when I was six).
5. Mr Brown will have to wait for two hours.
6. In a lot of/many offices the employees are not allowed to/may not smoke.
7. Jack must/has to look after his little brother today.
8. Susan will not/won't be able to play volleyball tomorrow.

Test
S. 72

Lösungen

Bits & Pieces
S. 74f.

Don't be caught speechless

Die folgenden Erklärungen sind Vorschläge:

1. Students/Pupils can get cheaper tickets if they show their student's card (ID card).
2. You mustn't go into the shop with rollerblades.
3. Children under eight can only go in with their mother or father.
4. Don't park here. If you do, you have to pay 80 Deutschmarks.

5. You put it on when you want to look at things under water. (snorkel)
6. It's a small piece of metal. You can fasten papers together with it. (paper clip)
7. You can dig holes into the ground with it. (spade)
8. It's an animal that lives in the sea. It is shaped like a star. (starfish)
9. Before it becomes a frog, it's a small creature with a black head and a long tail. (tadpole)
10. You can put something in it. It has got a wheel and two handles to lift and push it with. (wheelbarrow)
11. You need it if you want to receive lots of channels with your TV set. (satellite dish)
12. Athletes can jump very high with a long stick. (pole vaulting)

Lösungen Kapitel E

Exercise E1
S. 77

	Direct Speech Wörtliche Rede	Reported Speech Indirekte Rede
englischer Satz	Granny said: "I've lost my hearing aid."	Granny said she had lost her hearing aid.
deutscher Satz	Oma sagte: „Ich habe mein Hörgerät verloren."	Oma sagte, sie habe ihr Hörgerät verloren.

Exercise E 2
S. 78

	Direct Speech	Reported Speech
Verb Tense	needs Simple Present	needed Simple Past
Verb Tense	keeps Simple Present	kept Simple Past
Verb Tense	were wasted Simple Past	had been wasted Past Perfect
Verb Tense	have criticised Present Perfect	had criticised Past Perfect

Exercise E 3
S. 80

John's mother rang me up an hour ago. She said he was very sorry that he couldn't come to the party. She told me (that) he had been taken to hospital. There had been a football match at the school this morning. It had been the final of the school championship. She said (that) John had been running to get the ball when he had slipped, fallen and broken his ankle. Fortunately, his leg didn't hurt too badly. She also said he would stay in hospital for two days and he wouldn't be able to go to school for at least a week.

Lösungen

Exercise E 4
S. 81

1. He said (that) he had had a fight with a kangaroo.
2. David told Steve (that) the birds were flying north.
3. The man behind the desk said to David (that) he had tried to phone him at least ten times.
4. Helen said (that) she was sure that the two men would be found.
5. Jim said to the fireman (that) he needed a helmet and an axe.
6. He added (that) something had to be done.
7. The reporter said (that) nobody had been killed in the fire.

Exercise E 5
S. 83

1. Last week I visited Tony and his family. Tony said (that) there were no kids in their neighbourhood there.
2. He explained to me that his new school was more than five miles away.
3. And he said that his new classmates were really nice. Some of them had asked him to join the football team.
4. Then he told me (that) he was going to a school party the next day.
5. He also told me (that) he had been at the sports centre the previous day. He said it was great. He had never seen anything like that before.

Test
S. 84

"Yes, he called me the day before yesterday. He said he was ringing from Paris and it was a beautiful city. He told me that he had already seen the Eiffel Tower. The previous day/The day before they had gone to Versailles, that famous castle where the French kings had lived. Rupert said that there was gold everywhere, but he hadn't seen any bathrooms! Before that they had been to the Rhine Valley. He told me that they had to get up very early and that he was a little tired that day. He didn't feel like going to the opera that night! He also said he didn't have much time for writing postcards. He then explained to me that he would be in Rome the following/next day. A bus would take them to the most interesting sights. The last thing he said was that he had already taken hundreds of photos and that he had to go then because they were going to the Louvre."

Bits & Pieces
S. 86f.

How to use the dictionary

The gangsters were put behind bars.	*hinter Gitter*
He was engaged as a foreman.	*eingestellt*
He's not married but engaged.	*verlobt*
The line is engaged.	*Die Leitung ist besetzt.*
She was moved to tears.	*zu Tränen gerührt*
They moved to Munich.	*umziehen*
Don't move!	*sich bewegen*
What's the name of that famous pop star?	*Berühmtheit*
Starring Jodie Foster.	*in der Hauptrolle*
What do the stars say for today?	*Sterne, Horoskop*
We could see the moon and the stars.	*Sterne*
Your hands are dirty.	*Hände*
The child is in good hands.	*in guten Händen*
He worked as a farm-hand.	*Arbeiter*
The hour hand pointed to twelve.	*Zeiger*

Lösungen 165

Lösungen Kapitel F

Exercise F1
S. 89f.
There is somebody/someone/something in the car.
Give me some apples, please.
The camera must be somewhere.
I want something to drink.
There are some sausages left.
Somebody/Someone/Something is behind you.
Let's meet somewhere else.
I've just bought some cheese.
Something is wrong with my watch.

I don't know anybody/anyone here.
Is there any money left?
Has anybody/anyone got a hanky?
Have you seen him anywhere?
Is anything wrong?
I haven't got any sugar.
That doesn't make any sense.
Anything else?
I haven't got any friends.

Exercise F2
S. 90
1. The box is empty. There isn't anything in it.
2. There are some pencils on the writing-desk.
3. I need somebody/someone to help me with the washing-up.
4. You can phone me at any time.
5. Why don't we go somewhere else?
6. Can you see my purse anywhere?
7. Would you like some sandwiches?

Exercise F3
S. 91
1. There isn't anything in it.
2. We can't see it anywhere.
3. There aren't any stamps on the letter.
4. There wasn't anybody/anyone in the room.
5. He doesn't do anything all day.

Exercise F4
S. 92
1. Every
2. Each
3. each
4. every

baseball

Exercise F5
S. 93
1. many/a lot of
2. many/a lot of
3. a lot of
4. a lot of/lots of
5. much
6. a lot of/lots of

Exercise F 6
S. 94

1. little
2. few / a few
3. a little
4. a little
5. a few
6. a little

Test
S. 94 f.

1. Have you got much/a lot of work to do this afternoon?
2. I'm sorry, I haven't got any coke. But there is some milk in the fridge.
3. Gloria and Juliet go jogging together every Saturday.
4. Would you like some more tea?
5. You can take any bus from this stop.
6. Ms Redgrave has five cats. Each of her cats has a basket of its own.
7. We didn't have much time, so we only wrote a few/some postcards.
8. I was a little surprised ...

Bits & Pieces
S. 96 f.

Reading

| collector | *Sammler* | investigate | *untersuchen, Ermittlungen anstellen* |
| forgery | *Fälschung* | chemical | *chemisch* |

collector	collect	fame	famous
painting	paint	follower	follow
knowledge	know	changeable	change
meaningful	meaning	talkative	talk

chemical	*chemisch*	shoulder blade	*Schulterblatt*
information	*Information*	politician	*Politiker*
decoration	*Dekoration*	repair	*reparieren*
organize	*organisieren*	mass media	*Massenmedien*

Lösungen Kapitel G

Exercise G 1
S. 98

1. When Fred came to the site this morning three walls had already been finished. (true)
2. The cement was brought by a big cement mixer truck. (false)
3. Most of the windows have already been put in. (false)
4. Tomorrow the house will be finished. (false)
5. Heavy parts are lifted by a crane. (true)

Exercise G 2
S. 98

1. ... three walls had already been built. — Past Perfect
2. The cement was brought ... — Simple Past/Past Tense
3. ... the windows have already been put in. — Present Perfect
4. ... the house will be finished. — Future I
5. Heavy parts are lifted ... — Simple Present/Present Tense

Exercise G 3
S. 99f.
1. Engines are repaired.
2. Tyres are pumped up.
3. Brakes are checked.
4. Plugs are changed.
5. Tanks are filled./The tank is filled.
6. Cars are washed.
7. Windscreen wipers are repaired.
8. The oil is checked.

Exercise G 4
S. 101
1. The tyres are being changed.
2. The car is being washed.
3. The radio is being repaired.
4. The oil is being checked.
5. The lights are being tested.

Exercise G 5
S. 101
1. 52 persons were injured.
2. A bus was swept off the road.
3. Cars were overturned.
4. Trees were uprooted.
5. A bridge was destroyed.
6. The fire department was called twenty-seven times last night.

Exercise G 6
S. 102
1. The living room window has been broken.
2. The wardrobe has been opened.
3. All the clothes have been thrown on the floor.
4. Papers have been torn to pieces.
5. The TV set has been smashed up.
6. The silver candle sticks have been taken away.
7. The stamp collection has been stolen.
8. A bottle of whisky has been drunk.
9. The radio has been damaged.

Exercise G 7
S. 102
1. The window had been broken.
2. The wardrobe had been opened.
3. All the clothes had been thrown on the floor.
4. Papers had been torn to pieces.
5. The TV set had been smashed up.
6. The silver candle sticks had been taken away.
7. The stamp collection had been stolen.
8. A bottle of whisky had been drunk.
9. The radio had been damaged.

Exercise G 8
S. 104

Tom is writing a letter.	Active	Present
This machine was built in the USA.	Passive	Past
This parcel has been opened before.	Passive	Present Perfect
My friend has often been in London.	Active	Present Perfect
These recorders are made in Japan.	Passive	Present
We are making a doll.	Active	Present
The car was stolen last night.	Passive	Past
They were very happy.	Active	Past
The books were read by many people.	Passive	Past
Your father will be very angry.	Active	Future
A new hotel will be built in our street.	Passive	Future

Lösungen

Exercise G 9
S. 105

1. President Clinton's speech was printed by a lot of newspaper editors.
2. Ailwee Cave is visited by thousands of people every summer.
3. Fred was cut in two by the magician.
4. The wedding cake had been brought in by four waiters.
5. The new Madonna CD has already been bought by more that 200,000 people.
6. In 1998 the World Cup was won by the French team.
7. The exhibition will be opened by the mayor next Friday.

Exercise G 10
S. 107

1. Dogs must be kept on the lead.
2. The patients may be visited from 4 to 7 p. m.
3. The windows couldn't be opened.
4. Raw eggs must not be heated in the microwave.
5. Fred's leg had to be bandaged.
6. The paintings must not be photographed with a flash.
7. Oysters can be eaten raw.
8. Thank God the tooth didn't have to be pulled out.

Exercise G 11
S. 108

1. Tom was told an interesting story (by Granny).
2. Mr Smith had been sold the old Ford (by Mr Brown).
3. I was shown the way by a friendly gentleman.
4. Barbara has been sent a postcard from Australia (by one of her friends).
5. I was given a glass of orange juice by the stewardess.

Exercise G 12
S. 109

We will be picked up at Dublin airport.
We and our baggage will be taken to a guesthouse.
We will be given special cycling maps.
Our baggage will be transported from one guesthouse to the next.
Our rooms will be booked in advance.
We will be shown where to put our bikes.
We will be told where to find inns or coffee shops on the way.

Exercise G 13
S. 110

Past Perfect	Simple Past	Present Perfect	Simple Present	Future I
it had been stolen	it was stolen	it has been stolen	it is stolen	it will be stolen
he had been found	he was found	he has been found	he is found	he will be found
we had been asked	we were asked	we have been asked	we are asked	we will be asked
she had been seen	she was seen	she has been seen	she is seen	she will be seen
it had been sold	it was sold	it has been sold	it is sold	it will be sold
it had been made	it was made	it has been made	it is made	it will be made
it had been used	it was used	it has been used	it is used	it will be used
it had been written	it was written	it has been written	it is written	it will be written
they had been repaired	they were repaired	they have been repaired	they are repaired	they will be repaired

Lösungen 169

Test
S. 110f.

1. You will be picked up at the airport by Dad.
2. The car has often been repaired by Mr Brown himself.
3. Tea is drunk by people all over the world.
4. Mrs Barnes was offered a leading position by Skyline Enterprises.
5. The soundtrack had been written by David Bowie.
6. Four people and a cat had to be rescued from the burning house by the firemen.

The most exciting film that has ever been made!
America is attacked by dangerous creatures.
They were sent to take away all fast food restaurants.
If they can't be stopped, New York will be destroyed!
A hero must be found who will fight against these creatures.
He has been found: Fred, the Terminator!

Lösungen Kapitel H

Exercise H 1
S. 114f.

Past Perfect   Simple Past   Present Perfect   Simple Present

Conditional I   Future I

1. Kevin said to his cousin (that) he would meet him at the station.
2. Mrs Winter said (that) there was a new Mexican restaurant in Regent Street and (that) she had always wanted to try tortillas.
3. Susan said (that) they had gone on a cycling tour the weekend before. They hadn't got very far – it had started to rain ten minutes after they had left.
4. Tom said (that) the driver of the red Ford hadn't indicated. He had turned right rather abruptly.

Exercise H 2
S. 116

Present Tense ⟶ Past Tense
Past Tense ⟶ Past Perfect
Present Perfect ⟶ Past Perfect

Ja, die Zeitenfolge gilt in Fragesätzen genauso wie in Aussagesätzen.

Exercise H 3
S. 118f.

The first thing we wanted to know was how many hours per day the pupils spent in front of the "box".
We asked them what they had watched the day before/the previous day and if/whether there were any programmes they watched regularly.
We also wanted to find out if/whether they never/sometimes/often switched channels in the middle of a programme.
Of course we asked how many TV sets there were in their house/flat and if/whether they had got a TV set of their own.
Apart from that we wanted to know if/whether they had ever switched off the telly because they hadn't liked the programme and what they did during commercial breaks.

Exercise H 4
S. 119

1. He wanted to know if/whether I could sing.
2. He asked me in which plays I had already acted.
3. Then he asked me if/whether I was interested in a role and if I could come to the studio on Tuesday.

Exercise H 5
S. 122

1. First, Tim asked me to help him with his maths homework.
2. Then Mum wanted me to go to the supermarket and buy some eggs.
3. Grandma asked me to take a letter to the letterbox.
4. The worst thing was that Mum ordered me to tidy up my room.
5. Then Andy came in and asked me to draw an elephant for him.
6. When I said goodbye, Dad told me not to come home too late!

Exercise H 6
S. 122

Well, first Tim asked Ann to help him with his maths homework.
Then her mum wanted her to go to the supermarket and buy some eggs.
Her grandmother asked her to take a letter to the letterbox.
The worst thing was that her mum ordered her to tidy up her room.
Then Andy came in and asked her to draw an elephant for him.
When she said goodbye, her dad told her not to come home too late!

Exercise H 7
S. 123 f.

1. First he asked me why I had come/gone there.
2. I told him that I didn't feel very well.
3. After that he ordered me to stand up and bend my knees.
4. Then he wanted me to lie down on that couch.
5. He wanted to know if/whether I often drank alcohol.
6. I said to him that I had some bottles of beer every night.
7. He asked me where I had lunch and I told him (that) there was a canteen at my office and (that) I had a hot meal there every day.
8. He asked me if/whether you cooked a hot meal for me in the evening.
9. I answered that you did and that you were a splendid cook.
10. Then he wanted to know what I had done last weekend.
11. I told him that I had watched TV. There had been some good films on.
12. He then asked me when I had last gone for a walk and I replied that I didn't know. I had never liked doing that.
13. Then he said (he thought) he knew what was wrong with me: I ate too much.
14. He told me to have only one hot meal a day, to eat more fruit and (to try) to go for a walk every day. I would feel much better after that.

Test
S. 125

1. Shirley asked her friend if/whether he/she liked her dress.
2. The teacher said to Mary/told Mary to repeat the sentence.
3. The gangster ordered the old lady to give him her handbag.
4. The policeman asked the visitor where he had seen the man.
5. Lisa's new classmates wanted to know if/whether she had already been to the school cafeteria.
6. Mrs Scott told her little son not to throw the peas on the floor.
7. The boy told/wanted the dog to bring him the ball.
8. Paul asked Tim if/whether he was tired.
9. Fiona asked her aunt when she would go on holiday this/that year.
10. Mr White told his daughter not to use his tie as a belt.

Lösungen 171

Lösungen Kapitel I

Exercise I 1
S. 131
1. Barbara's brother
2. the bird's nest
3. Canada's new president
4. the boy's feet
5. men's socks
6. the pig's head
7. a one hour's break
8. children's toys
9. Germany's biggest city
10. our neighbour's dog

Exercise I 2
S. 132
1. the Millers' new car
2. the horses' ears
3. the twins' jackets
4. a two hours' delay
5. dogs' biscuits
6. my parents' room
7. the Greens' garden
8. a four hours' drive
9. my sisters' bikes
10. the rabbits' ears

Exercise I 3
S. 133
1. the name of the street/road
2. the roofs of the houses
3. the roots of the trees
4. the car of the people who/that moved in last week
5. the colour of my new umbrella
6. the names of the animals that/which live in Australia

Exercise I 4
S. 135
1. On Monday morning she went to the baker's and to the butcher's.
2. In the afternoon she was at the dentist's and at the chemist's.
3. She spent (the) Tuesday morning at the hairdresser's.
4. A lady asked: "Is the red sports car yours?"
   Mrs Silverstone answered: "No, it's not mine. It's my brother's."
5. From Wednesday till Saturday she stayed at her sister's.

Exercise I 5
S. 136
1. That's Julie, a friend of mine from Australia.
2. That's Pete. A neighbour of his is watering the flowers!
3. Charlie's uncle is a fireman. That's Charlie with some colleagues of his uncle's.
4. And that's Maggie. Juggling is a great hobby of hers.

Lösungen

Exercise 16
S. 137

1. The Millers' new car has got seats for seven people.
2. The walls of my room are decorated with lots of posters.
3. A friend of mine celebrated his birthday last Saturday.
4. Linda's brother broke his leg yesterday.
5. We have a twenty minutes' break at 10.30.
6. The roof of our neighbour's house has to be repaired.
7. Is that the purse of the lady with the two poodles?
8. That's not Jane's jacket, it's Diana's./That's not Diana's jacket, it's Jane's.
9. Children's clothes are rather expensive in this shop.
10. The birds' feathers were glittering in the sun.
11. My sister had to go to the dentist's this morning.
12. The Empire State Building is one of America's highest skyscrapers.

Test
S. 138

1. in three weeks' time
2. Her father's cousin
3. the girls' dogs
4. a photo of the house
5. The name of the girl
6. her sister's name
7. a twenty hours' flight
8. A friend of hers/One of her friends
9. At the doctor's
10. Australia's wildlife/Australia's animals

Mentor Lernhilfen für die 8.–10. Klasse.
Die haben's drauf.

Deutsch

Vorsicht Fehler! Deutsch (63535-2)

Diktate, ab 8. Klasse
Schülerbuch mit Elternteil (63513-1)
Multimedia-CD-ROM (63524-7)

Neue Rechtschreibung spielerisch
Multimedia-CD-ROM (63534-4)

Grammatik, 7./8. Klasse (63514-X)

Aufsatzschreiben, 8.–10. Klasse (2 Bände)
Inhaltsangabe, Charakteristik, Referat (63519-0)
Gedichtinterpretation, Erörterung (63520-4)

Englisch

Vorsicht Fehler! Englisch (63560-3)

Keep it up! 7./8. Klasse (2 Bände)
Wortschatz und Grammatik (63545-X, 63546-8)

The Final Touch, 9./10. Klasse (2 Bände)
Indirekte Rede, Gerundium u.a. (63550-6)
Relativsätze, Simple Past, Partizip u.a. (63551-4)

Französisch

Vorsicht Fehler! Französisch (63585-9)

Ça alors! (4 Bände)
Verbformen, Verneinung, Passé composé,
Teilungsartikel u.a.(1./2. Jahr, 63565-4)

Imparfait, Fragesätze, Objekt- u. Relativpronomen u.a. (ab 2. Jahr, 63566-2)

Futur u. Konditional, indirekte Rede,
Adverb u.a (ab 3. Jahr,.63567-0)

Accord, Subjonctif, Gérondif, Participe présent
(ab 3./4.Jahr, 63568-9)

(ISBN-Vorspann zur Bestellnummer: 3-580-)

**Und alles selbstverständlich in neuer Rechtschreibung.
Fragen Sie in Ihrer Buchhandlung danach!**

Latein

Grammatik mit Spaß! ab 2. Jahr (63591-3)

Satzbau mit System, 3./4. Jahr (63592-1)

Mathematik

Algebra 7./8. Klasse (2 Bände)
Brüche, Zinsen, Prozente u. a. (63620-0)
Binome, Funktionen, Stochastik u. a. (63621-9)

Algebra 9./10. Klasse (2 Bände)
Wurzeln, Parabeln, quadratische Gleichungen
(63630-8)
Potenzfunktionen, Stochastik u. a. (63631-6)

Geometrie 7./8. Klasse (2 Bände)
Spiegelung, Drehung, Vektoren u. a. (63625-1)
Dreieck, Gerade, Flächen u. a. (63626-X)

Geometrie 9./10. Klasse (2 Bände)
Zentrische Streckung u. a. (63635-9)
Trigonometrie, Vektorrechnung u. a. (63636-7)

Biologie

Humanbiologie, 9.–11. Klasse
(in alter Rechtschreibung, 64640-0)

Physik

Physik, Mittelstufe (2 Bände)
Mechanik, Wärmelehre, Akustik u.a. (63660-X)
Optik, Magnetismus, Elektrizität u.a. (63661-8)

Chemie

Chemie, Grundwissen (2 Bände)
Allgemeine u. anorganische Chemie (63675-8)
Organische Chemie (63676-6)

Mentor
Eine Klasse besser.

Bücher und CD-ROMs für Rechtschreibung und Diktat
Natürlich von Mentor.

Rechtschreibung und Diktat ab 4. Klasse

Für einen erfolgreichen Wechsel in weiterführende Schulen

In 33 Tagen durch das Land Fehlerlos
Rechtschreibung 4. Klasse (63500-X)

Endlich sicher beim Diktat
Diktat 4. Klasse (63502-6)

Diktate 5.–8. Klasse Mit starken Texten zum Erfolg

Wahlweise als Schülerbuch mit Elternteil oder als Multimedia-CD-ROM mit Korrekturfunktion

Diktate 5. Klasse
Buch mit Elternteil (63506-9)
CD-ROM (63521-2)

Diktate 6. Klasse
Buch mit Elternteil (63508-5)
CD-ROM (63522-0)

Diktate 7. Klasse
Buch mit Elternteil (63512-3)
CD-ROM (63523-9)

Diktate ab 8. Klasse
Buch mit Elternteil (63513-1)
CD-ROM (63524-7)

(ISBN-Vorspann: 3-580-)

Und alles selbstverständlich in neuer Rechtschreibung!
Fragen Sie in Ihrer Buchhandlung danach!

Rechtschreibung 5.–7. Klasse

Rechtschreiben intensiv: spannende Geschichten und Übungen rund um die Kommissarin Alice Lux

Rechtschreib-Krimis 1
Buchstaben und Laute, Worttrennung
(63510-7)

Rechtschreib-Krimis 2
Groß oder klein, zusammen oder getrennt, Komma oder nicht? (63511-5)

Neue Rechtschreibung für Umsteiger

Für Jugendliche und Erwachsene, die zur neuen Rechtschreibung noch Fragen haben ...

Neue Rechtschreibung spielerisch
Regeln, Merkhilfen und Übungen
CD-ROM (63534-4)

Das Wichtigste auf einen Blick
Schautafel zur neuen Rechtschreibung
Großformat A0 (63533-6)

Mentor
Eine Klasse besser.